THE FWBO AND
'PROTESTANT BUDDHISM'
AN AFFIRMATION AND A PROTEST

For thirty-five years Sangharakshita has been playing an important part in the spread of Buddhism throughout the modern world. He is head of the Western Buddhist Order (Trailokya Bauddha Mahasangha), and is actively engaged in what is now an international Buddhist movement with centres in thirteen countries worldwide. When not visiting centres he is based at a community in Norfolk. His writings are available in eleven languages.

Also by Sangharakshita:
Messengers from Tibet and Other Poems
A Survey of Buddhism
Flame in Darkness
The Enchanted Heart
The Three Jewels
Crossing the Stream
The Essence of Zen
The Path of the Inner Life
The Thousand-Petalled Lotus
Human Enlightenment
The Religion of Art
The Ten Pillars of Buddhism
The Eternal Legacy
Travel Letters
Alternative Traditions
Conquering New Worlds
Ambedkar and Buddhism
The History of My Going for Refuge
The Taste of Freedom
New Currents in Western Buddhism
A Guide to the Buddhist Path
Learning to Walk
Vision and Transformation
The Buddha's Victory
Facing Mount Kanchenjunga

The Meaning of Orthodoxy in Buddhism
Mind—Reactive and Creative
Aspects of Buddhist Morality
Buddhism and Blasphemy
Buddhism, World Peace, and Nuclear War
The Bodhisattva: Evolution and Self-Transcendence
The Glory of the Literary World
Going For Refuge
The Caves of Bhaja
My Relation to the Order
Hercules and the Birds and Other Poems

SANGHARAKSHITA **THE FWBO AND
'PROTESTANT BUDDHISM'**
AN AFFIRMATION AND A PROTEST

WINDHORSE PUBLICATIONS

Published by Windhorse Publications
136 Renfield Street
Glasgow G2 3AU

Cover design Dhammarati

Printed by Dotesios Ltd,
Trowbridge, Wiltshire

British Library Cataloguing in Publication Data.
A catalogue record for this book is available from the British Library

ISBN 0-904766-60-8

PREFACE

OVER RECENT DECADES thousands of Westerners have
embraced Buddhism. Or, at least, they think they have.

In growing numbers, they have been attending meetings, clas-
ses, courses, and retreats led by Buddhist teachers at Buddhist
centres. They have been learning to meditate, gauging the moral
worth of their actions by the light of precepts originally
prescribed by the Buddha, and turning to the Buddhist scriptures for advice, guidance, and inspiration. Many have received
ordination and initiation into one branch or another of the
Buddhist sangha, and ever more of them have been devoting
their lives to teaching the Dharma and to creating the institutions which will serve as channels for Buddhist practice and
Buddhist ways of life for years to come. In doing so, most of
them have no doubt thought a lot about the issues involved in
making a set of teachings historically associated with the East
relevant not only to their own lives but to the moral, cultural,
and spiritual life of the West as well.

To be involved in this process of 'translation'—whether in
one's own inner life as a practising Buddhist or as an active
member of the Buddhist spiritual community engaged in the
task of 'bringing the Dharma to the West'—must be one of the
most exciting adventures available today in the life of the spirit.

Well, that is how it feels. But are we fooling ourselves? Are we
really Buddhists? Is our Buddhism really Buddhism? Is it instead possible that we are unwittingly playing out the latest act
in a drama that began, not in Bodh Gaya some 2,500 years ago,
but in sixteenth century Europe, something that has more to do
with the history and development of Christianity than with
Buddhism?

It would certainly be hard to define as a Buddhist someone who was not alive to the principle that 'nothing arises except in dependence upon conditions'. Our thoughts, moods, actions, and beliefs of today are in some way inextricably linked to those of yesterday. Inevitably we Westerners are bringing to our Buddhism an unknown quantity of assumptions, expectations, hopes, and fears that we picked up with our early Christian conditioning—even when that consisted of little more than socialization into a nominally Christian society. But, as any serious Buddhist practitioner knows, the detection of these stowaway attitudes provides some of the most exciting moments on the journey of self-discovery. Indeed, so central to the spiritual life of the individual, and to the integrity of a youthful Western Buddhist community, is the exposure of such patterns and prejudices that any help we can get from those who see us more clearly than we see ourselves is a priceless gift.

So it was hard not to turn to Philip Mellor's essay, 'Protestant Buddhism? The Cultural Translation of Buddhism in England', without a tingle of anticipation. Dr Mellor was claiming to have discovered that, on the evidence provided by the Friends of the Western Buddhist Order (FWBO) and the English Sangha, we English Buddhists are so deeply enmeshed in the attitudes and ideas of the Protestant Christian world from which we emerged that Buddhism in England is 'a problematic category for the analyst'—i.e. it isn't what it thinks it is, and we Buddhists aren't what we think we are. Strong stuff indeed, and potentially important grist to our mill.

Taken on its own terms by the disinterested academic reader to whom the essay is addressed, Mellor's argument must seem thoroughly convincing. To test his hypothesis that 'Christian discourses and forms of life continue to have an observable influence on English Buddhism', Mellor compares attitudes and approaches to such issues as 'the burden of self', tradition, modernism, morality, ritual, and culture found within the FWBO and the English Sangha to those normally associated with the

Protestant Christian outlook.

Like trained seals, the two Buddhist movements perform magnificently (though the FWBO rather outshines its companion). There doesn't seem to be a ball that Mellor can throw at them that they will not obligingly catch and balance on their noses. The degree to which the case-studies confirm the theory is almost dizzying. And at a time when so many people in the Christian and academic worlds are wondering (for their own reasons) why Westerners are turning to Oriental religions, sects, and cults, Mellor's paper, for all its brevity, raises aloft the spectre of a veritable holy grail. It is the sort of thing that careers are built on.

What the disinterested reader would not know, unfortunately, is that the FWBO described in the essay, with its rather self-obsessed membership under the spell of a charismatic leader, its self-consciously modern contempt for tradition and culture, its indifferent or permissive attitude to morality, its distain for ritual, its insignificant presence in India, and so on, bears no relation to the FWBO as it is known and nurtured by those who are involved with it.

Is one, in feeling compelled to draw attention to this broadside of misrepresentations, merely revealing the predictable touchiness of one whose Buddhist foundations are both shallow and shaky? Is one, in disagreeing with Mellor's assessments, merely recoiling from truths that are hard to bear—and thus demonstrating one's inability to be objective about the facts when seen, for a change, through the detached eyes of an academic? Is Mellor completely free of his own value judgements and not being as critical as he may seem to his subjects? Is he substantially correct in his perceptions, and thus in his conclusions? 'Yes,' says Mellor. 'No,' say we.

On reading the essay, Dharmachari Kulananda of the FWBO's Liaison Office wrote to the magazine that had published it, highlighting a number or errors and misrepresentations. A subsequent, published reply by Mellor more or less took the attitude outlined above. Kulananda's very seeing of errors, and his desire to point them out, merely proved that these matters are best left to the scholars who can be objective about them.

Meanwhile, Sangharakshita, the FWBO's founder, was already engaged in a rather different literary endeavour. He had found some of Mellor's arguments, sources, and interpretations so stimulating that he had embarked upon a virtual word-by-word critical commentary on the work aiming, above all, to explore the issues that it had unearthed. The fruits of his labour are before you.

It has to be said that this book is not for the squeamish. It will not appeal to those who think that Buddhist tolerance involves an uncritical acceptance of everything that anyone cares to say about anything. Inevitably Sangharakshita has had to deal— often, and sometimes at length—with Mellor's errors and mis-judgements, an irksome task for someone whose ideals and life's work have been so carelessly distorted. Sangharakshita's concern is with the deeper issues, but if Mellor's treatment of his theme has dictated that an 'adversarial' approach is the only way to join in, then so be it.

The FWBO is growing and developing all the time. Even while Sangharakshita has been engaged in writing this book new FWBO centres, communities, and Right Livelihood businesses have come to life. Another fifty or so men and women (from England, Scotland, New Zealand, India, Germany, and Spain) have joined the Western Buddhist Order. As it grows and plays a more significant part in the spiritual and cultural life of the modern world, the FWBO will increasingly draw attention to it-self. It is bound to become a regular object of study and com-ment. It would therefore be better for all concerned if anyone attempting to present the FWBO in any context and for any reason did so accurately and sensitively. If Sangharakshita's occasionally vigorous wielding of Manjushri's sword in the following pages will have the effect of putting future commen-tators on their mettle then so much the better.

But, for now, Dr Mellor is to be thanked. In his essay he has highlighted—and thus invited comment upon—a series of issues that are of vital importance to anyone concerned with the cultural translation of Buddhism not only in England but in the modern world. That in doing so he should have woven a sub-text replete with the sort of assumptions and confusions that so often cloud the discussion of these themes, even within the Buddhist world—and thus provided Sangharakshita with an opportunity to speak out—is, I think, a considerable bonus. I hope you will agree.

Nagabodhi
Vimalakula Community
June 1992

MANJUSRI, the bodhisattva who as the embodiment of
wisdom presides over the propagation of the Dharma, is
iconographically represented not only as bearing in his left
hand a lotus blossom upon whose open petals rests a book,
the Scriptures of Perfect Wisdom, but also as wielding with
his right hand a flaming sword. While the first symbolizes
the establishment of Truth the second symbolizes the
destruction of untruth, that is to say, of those doctrines
which do not constitute a basis for the attainment
of the transcendental Path.

A Survey of Buddhism

WRITING is an excellent means of awakening in every man
the system slumbering within him; and everyone who has
ever written will have discovered that writing always
awakens something which, though it lay within us, we
failed clearly to recognize before.

Georg Christoph Lichtenberg (1742–99)

IN FEBRUARY 1986 I received a letter from a certain Philip Mellor. 'I am at the University of Manchester,' he wrote, 'where I am working on a Ph.D. on the cultural transference of Buddhism into the West in the Department of Comparative Religion, where my supervisor is Dr Alan Williams. I am concerned with the development of, and modifications to, Buddhism in this country. In the light of your personal commitment to Buddhism, your involvement with the English Sangha Trust in the 1960s, and the development of your own Friends of the Western Buddhist Order I consider it extremely important for my work to be able to talk to you. First of all I would like to hear your first hand account of this period of Buddhism in this country, and second, I would appreciate your general thoughts on the wider topic of cultural transference or translation in terms of the Western context within which Buddhism has now to operate.' Naturally I agreed to Mr Mellor's request, and six or seven weeks later, on 16 April, we met at Padmaloka, my personal headquarters near Norwich. In the course of the interview, which lasted for about two hours and which he tape-recorded, Mr Mellor questioned me about the circumstances in which I returned to Britain in 1964, about why the English Sangha Trust refused, two years later, to renew their invitation to me to teach at the Hampstead Buddhist Vihara, about Christmas Humphreys's attitude to the FWBO, about the severing of the Buddhist Society's link with Theosophy after Humphreys's death, and about the relation between the Western Buddhist Order and the earlier, abortive organization of that name started by the Venerable Robert Stuart Clifton. Only towards the end of the interview did he ask me for my thoughts on 'the wider topic of cultural transference or translation in terms of the Western context within which Buddhism has now to operate' and on what he saw as differences between the Friends of the Western Buddhist Order (FWBO) and the English Sangha, i.e. the Theravadin community closely related to the forest monasteries of Ajahn Chah in Thailand.

A year and two months after our meeting, Mr Mellor sent me a copy of the transcription of the interview, at the same time returning a copy of *The Thousand-Petalled Lotus* that had been lent to him. That was four years ago. Thereafter I heard nothing from Mr Mellor and, occupied as I was with the actual task of cultural transference of Buddhism into the West, thought no more of him and his Ph.D.

Early this year, however, there reached me reports to the effect that the FWBO was being held up, in certain academic circles in Britain, as an example of 'Protestant Buddhism'. These reports eventually came to centre on an article which, it was said, had appeared in the January 1991 issue of the journal *Religion* (not to be confused with *Religion Today*), published by the Department of Religious Studies, Lancaster University. With some difficulty I managed to obtain a copy. It was entitled 'Protestant Buddhism? The Cultural Translation of Buddhism in England' and was by Philip A. Mellor, the man who had interviewed me five years earlier. He had recently obtained his Ph.D. from the Faculty of Theology at the University of Manchester with a thesis dealing with problems of theory and method in the study of contemporary religion (so a note subjoined to the text informed the reader), and was now a lecturer in the Department of Theology and Religious Studies at the Liverpool Institute of Higher Education.

The article proved to be something of a disappointment. Not that I had expected the author to be particularly sympathetic to the FWBO or to agree with all my 'thoughts' on the cultural transference or translation of Buddhism. It was a disappointment because it contained a great deal of theory and methodology but very little in the way of actual information about the FWBO, even though the FWBO was one of the two 'English' Buddhist groups on which the author professed to concentrate in his discussion of the relationship of English Buddhism with Protestant Christian perspectives, the other group being the English Sangha. Worse still, such information as the article did provide was either so simplistic and selective as to give quite a misleading impression of the FWBO or simply erroneous. In some cases views were attributed to the FWBO which were the exact opposite of those it actually holds. What could be done to set the record straight? At my suggestion Dharmachari Kulananda drafted a reply to Philip Mellor's article for publication in *Religion*.[1] In this reply, which ran to 2,500 words, Kulananda confined himself to correcting some of the factual errors in Mellor's characterization of the FWBO—in itself a sufficiently extensive undertaking. This would suffice, I hoped, to set the record straight at least on matters of fact and at least so far as the (mainly academic) readership of the journal was concerned. But what of those larger theoretical and methodological questions in the context of which Mellor had made his mistakes about the FWBO and which were, perhaps, responsible for his Procrustean distortions of FWBO teaching and practice? Surely something should be done about *them*! In the end I decided to write a response of my own to Mellor's article. Not a reply but a response. I would look at some of the theoretical and methodological questions raised by his article, either explicitly or by implication. I would look at them in my own way, that is, I would look at them as a (Western) Buddhist, without any pretence of adopting an 'objective' approach to Buddhism and without allowing myself to be restrained by considerations of academic propriety.

Mellor's article is divided into five sections. These are headed, respectively: 'The Burden of Self', 'Protestantism and Buddhism', 'Modernism and Buddhism', 'Culture and Buddhism', and 'The Cultural Translation of Buddhism'. My response will be similarly divided, though I shall not be looking at all the questions raised by the article, nor looking at them systematically; neither shall I be concerned to correct factual errors about the FWBO, except where these are particularly flagrant. At times I may permit myself to digress, or take advantage of an opportunity to clarify my position on certain topics beyond the immediate requirements of the discussion. But before the first section of Mellor's article there comes an introductory paragraph, the contents of which also need to be scrutinized. I give the paragraph in full.

'In the discussion that follows I suggest that the development of Buddhism in England is not necessarily an indicator of a complete disenchantment with western, Christian religious positions. I argue that this is a simplification of the real situation. Rather than understanding English Buddhism as a phenomenon completely at odds with western religious traditions, I consider a number of ways in which it participates in them. Religions are not free-floating, metaphysical phenomena impervious to all social, intellectual and political conditions. On the contrary, it is my contention that religions are always and everywhere embedded in social and cultural realities. The development of new forms of religious life in a particular culture is not necessarily a signifier of the collapse of the constraining forces of social structures and systems, but of these structures and systems enabling new developments to take place. As I shall note, there are many features in contemporary English Buddhism that indicate a complex relationship with Protestant Christian perspectives. I concentrate my discussion on the Friends of the Western Buddhist Order (FWBO), a consciously "western" Buddhist group, and the English Sangha, a community closely related to the forest monasteries of Ajahn Chah in Thailand. The two groups are linked by the fact that neither are ethnic and that Sangharakshita, the founder and leader of the FWBO, also led the English Sangha for a brief period in the 1960s before founding the FWBO. Nevertheless, they demonstrate markedly different visions of how Buddhism should be understood and practised in the west. In the discussion of these two approaches I also intend to draw some general conclusions about the difficulties of translating an eastern religious tradition into a western cultural environment.'

Here we are confronted by a number of ambiguities. The more serious of them relate to the expressions 'English Buddhism' and 'western religious traditions', to the relations between religions and social and cultural realities, and to the description of the FWBO as a consciously 'western' group.

1 At the very beginning of my interview with Philip Mellor (as by him transcribed) I spoke of my having had no intention of coming back to Britain. In this introductory paragraph, however, Mellor speaks of 'Buddhism in *England*' and '*English* Buddhism', as he in fact does throughout the article, in the body of which he also speaks, repeatedly, of *English* Buddhists. But 'England' is no more equivalent to 'Britain' than 'English' is to 'British'. Is Mellor so remote from social and cultural realities as to be unaware of this and unaware, therefore, that a discussion of the development of Buddhism in England is by no means the same thing as a discussion of the development of Buddhism in Britain? Apparently he is. At least he gives no indication of *not* being unaware. He is unaware that there are native-born Buddhists in Scotland, for example, who, while they might be happy for Buddhism in Scotland to be treated as part of Buddhism in Britain, and for themselves to be described as British Buddhists, would certainly object to Buddhism in Scotland being treated as part of Buddhism in *England* and themselves described as *English* Buddhists. The point is relevant to a discussion of the Friends of the Western Buddhist Order (FWBO) and cultural translation, the reason being that the FWBO has a presence not only in England but also in Scotland and Wales, as well as having a substantial number of Scots Order members and Mitras living and working in England. (I shall discuss the question of the extent to which the FWBO can be regarded as English later on.) It is also relevant in view of Mellor's contention that 'religions are always and everywhere embedded in social and cultural realities.' Scottish social and cultural realities are not the same as those in England (Scotland has its own educational system, for example). A discussion of the FWBO and cultural translation therefore needs to take into account the fact that the realities in which the FWBO are 'embedded' are not exclusively English, any more than the FWBO itself, even within the United Kingdom, is a purely English phenomenon.

2 'Buddhism in England' and 'Buddhism in Britain' are not the only expressions Mellor regards as synonymous. The same treatment is given to 'western, Christian religious positions' and 'western religious traditions'. Having in the first sentence of his introductory paragraph spoken of the development of Buddhism in England being not necessarily an indicator of complete disenchantment with western, Christian religious positions, in the next sentence but one he speaks of his refusal to understand English Buddhism as a phenomenon completely at odds with western religious traditions. But 'Christian religious positions' (apparently Mellor's euphemism for Christian dogmas) cannot really be equated with 'western religious traditions'. Besides the traditions of classical antiquity, such as Mithraism, Gnosticism, Hermeticism, and Neoplatonism in its more religious aspect, there are Alchemy, Theosophy, Rosicrucianism, and Freemasonry. There are, in fact, all the various alternative traditions of the West which, after surviving 'underground' in an attenuated form, or being reconstituted from the literary remains that became available at the time of the Renaissance, have come to constitute an increasingly serious challenge to Christianity. With these alternative traditions Buddhism in England is not necessarily 'disenchanted' in the way that it is with 'western, Christian religious positions'; nor is the phenomenon of English Buddhism by any means 'completely at odds' with them. In a paper on 'My Relation to the Order' I speak of Neoplatonism as being the major spiritual tradition of the West, just as Buddhism is the major spiritual tradition of the East, and make the point that Buddhists can no more afford to ignore Neoplatonism than Neoplatonists (should there be any left) can afford to ignore Buddhism.[2] I would go farther than that. Having read, in the course of the last few years, all the major surviving texts of Neoplatonism, from Plotinus to Proclus, I have come to the conclusion that such affinities as exist between Buddhism and the religious traditions of the West are to be found in Neoplatonism rather than in Christianity, notwithstanding the fact that Christian theology and mysticism are both deeply indebted to Neoplatonism. This can, of course, be discounted as a minority view; but in point of fact there has been very little comparative study of Buddhism and Neoplatonism. We have a paper on 'Plotinus and Vijñānavāda Buddhism' and a paper which, despite being headed 'Phraseology and Imagery in Plotinus and Indian Thought', is devoted mainly to Neoplatonic and Indian ideas on divine activity, in particular, the views of Plotinus and those expressed in the Mahayana Buddhist work *Uttaratantra* or *Ratnagotravibhāga*—and that is about all.[3] There can, however, be little doubt that Westerners attracted to Buddhism are often sympathetically disposed, at the same time, to the alternative traditions of the West, especially as mediated by the writings of Carl Gustav Jung, Frances A. Yates, and Edgar Wind.

Thus there is no question of English Buddhism being 'completely at odds' with western religious traditions, in the sense of being at odds with Christianity *and* the alternative traditions of the West. What English Buddhism is at odds with, whether completely or otherwise, is Christianity, or, in Mellor's euphemistic phrase, 'Christian religious positions'. English Buddhism denies what Christianity affirms, though that denial is incidental to its own spiritual affirmations and though individual English Buddhists may not be sufficiently informed about Christianity to be aware that they are, in effect, denying its fundamental teachings. But how strange it is that in speaking of the relation between the development of Buddhism in England/English Buddhism on the one hand and western, Christian religious positions/western religious traditions on the other, Mellor should make use of such expressions as 'at odds with' and 'disenchanted'! According to *Collins Dictionary* 'at odds' means 'on bad terms' (the *Concise Oxford* has 'variance, strife'). Surely to speak of serious religious and philosophical differences in this way is to reduce them to the level of a personal misunderstanding or even a personal quarrel. It is to trivialize the important issues involved. I am reminded of the line that well-meaning Christian friends used to take with me on learning that, though a Buddhist monk, I had been born into a (nominally) Christian family. 'Oh we *quite* understand!' they would exclaim sympathetically. 'You must have had a *very* bad experience of Christians (or of the Church). But you mustn't judge Christianity by Christians, you know. That wouldn't be fair.' But I didn't judge Christianity by Christians, I used to tell them. My experience of Christians had been quite positive. I judged Christianity by its teachings, and the reason I was a Buddhist and not a Christian (apart from the overwhelming appeal of Buddhism itself) was that I could not accept those teachings. Sometimes I added, for good measure, that my experience of Buddhists (I was then living in the East) had been much worse than my experience of Christians and that if my faith in Buddhism had depended on a positive experience of Buddhists I probably would have given up Buddhism long ago. What my well-meaning Christian friends were doing, and what Mellor it fact does, can be described as an attempt to 'personalize' matters of principle, and it is this tendency to personalization and subjectivization that is so prominent a feature of that very modernism of which, in the third section of his article, he is quick to accuse the FWBO.

It is the same with 'disenchant', defined by *Collins* as 'to free from or as if from enchantment; disillusion.' In speaking of 'disenchantment with western, Christian religious positions' Mellor is again personalizing matters of principle, thereby suggesting that to the extent that the development of Buddhism in England is due to such disenchantment it is due to a subjective, irrational disappointment with Christianity rather than being the result, as it is in the case of many English Buddhists, of a critical awareness of the inadequacies of that religion. Disenchantment in any case implies a previous state of enchantment. There are not a few English Buddhists who cannot be said to have been disenchanted with Christianity for the simple reason that they were never enchanted with it in the first place, either because they were brought up as Humanists, or Jews, or Theosophists, or Marxists, or because they were raised in an environment free from religious influences. I would also have thought that to speak of disengagement from Christianity in terms of disenchantment was rather unfortunate, at any rate from the Christian point of view, conjuring up as the expression does an image of Christianity as a Circean figure from whose spells the ex-Christian has succeeded in breaking free.

3 'Religions,' says Mellor, 'are not free-floating, metaphysical phenomena impervious to all social, intellectual and political conditions.' Of course they are not, and I very much doubt if there is anyone who really thinks they are. Mellor presumably states the rejected view in such extreme terms simply in order to make his own contrary—and no less extreme—view that 'religions are always and everywhere embedded in social and cultural realities' seem moderate and reasonable. But is it so reasonable—or so clear—as it appears? The word embedded means to be 'fixed firmly and deeply in the surrounding mass' or to be 'surrounded closely' (*Collins*), and it is therefore not the most appropriate term to use in connection with the kind of relation that obtains between religions and what Mellor calls social and cultural realities. An object may be fixed firmly and deeply in a surrounding mass in two ways. It may be fixed in it in such a way that only a part of it is enclosed by the surrounding mass (the relation of lotus plant to mud), or it may be fixed in it in such a way that it is completely enclosed by that mass (the relation of fossil to rock). If religions really are 'always and everywhere' embedded in social and cultural realities in the sense of being completely enclosed by those realities it follows that religions have only a social and cultural existence and that, earth-bound phenomena that they are, they possess no supra-social, supra-cultural, spiritual dimension. English Buddhism is not committed to such a view of religions, least of all to such a view of Buddhism itself. Whether it is Mellor's own view is not clear, but since in describing the relation between religions and social and cultural realities he makes use of a term which is, as we have seen, ambiguous, we cannot assume that it is *not* his own view.

There is a similar ambiguity in Mellor's description of the relation between new forms of religious life and the social structures and systems of the culture in which they arise. Having contended that, far from being free-floating metaphysical phenomena, religions are always and everywhere embedded in social and cultural realities, he goes on to say, 'The development of new forms of religious life in a particular culture in not necessarily a signifier of the collapse of the constraining forces of social structures and systems, but of these structures and systems enabling new developments to take place.' The ambiguity is in the word enabling. In what sense do the social structures and systems of an existing culture positively 'enable' new developments to take place? Can it really be said that they 'provide [new forms of religious life] with adequate power, means, opportunity, or authority' to develop (*Collins*), or even that they make such developments 'possible or easy' (the secondary meaning of the word)? More often than not, the old structures and systems make the development of new forms of religious life possible—though not necessarily easy—only in the negative sense of not actually getting in the latter's way, and the reason they do not get in their way is that they no longer are in a position to do so. In the case of the new form of religious life that is English Buddhism, the 'constraining forces' of the structures and systems of the particular culture in which it has developed have been largely Christian, and it was only with the virtual 'collapse' of those forces that Buddhism could develop here. We all know what would have happened if a Sinhalese monk had tried to preach his non-theistic religion in fifteenth century (Catholic) Oxford, or if a Tibetan lama had attempted to do the same thing in seventeenth century (Puritan/Anglican) London. This is not to say that there are not in English culture structures which make the development of Buddhism in England easier, at least organizationally speaking. There is the Charity Commission, for example, registration with which exempts Christian and non-Christian bodies alike from taxation. But what really enables new developments like English Buddhism to take place, in the sense of making them possible by default, is the virtual collapse of our largely Christian constraining forces—a collapse of which the existence of structures like the Charity Commission is itself a 'signifier'.

4 According to Mellor, the FWBO is 'a consciously "western" Buddhist group' (it is not clear what the inverted commas are meant to convey). At the same time the FWBO is one of the two groups on which he concentrates his discussion of the 'complex relationship' between contemporary *English* Buddhism and Protestant Christian perspectives. Having treated 'English Buddhism' and 'English Buddhists' as equivalent to 'British Buddhism' and 'British Buddhists', he now proceeds to treat '"western" Buddhist group' as equivalent to 'English Buddhist group'. This is not only ambiguous but positively confusing. I shall therefore try to make it clear in what sense, and to what

extent, the FWBO is western, with or without the mysterious inverted commas, and in what sense, and to what extent, it is
English. This will enable us to see what Mellor is discussing—or
ought to be discussing—when he discusses the FWBO.

In the latter part of my interview with Mellor I emphasized
that, whether in India or elsewhere, I had been concerned only
to teach the Dharma, so far as I understood it. There was no
question of my teaching an Eastern Buddhism in the East and a
Western Buddhism in the West, even though I found on my
return to Britain that certain ways of presenting things were
more effective or comprehensible in the West than others, or that
certain practices and observances were not acceptable here. 'So I
proceeded on a purely empirical, experimental basis,' I explained. 'I was just concerned to teach the Dharma, not any
Western version of it—far from it I was [and still am] very tradi-
tionally-minded. I'm not trying to "adapt" the Dharma; I'm just
trying to make it understandable.... If one can talk of a Western
Buddhism [at all] it is only in the sense of a form in which the
Dharma can be understood and practised in modern Western
society. [So far as I am concerned] it is not an "interpretation" of
the Dharma.' Surprisingly, Mellor makes no reference to this
passage from our interview, though he quotes the immediately
following passage in which I distinguish between Tradition with
a capital T and tradition with a small T—a passage which really
needs to be read in the light of my previous remarks about my
own teaching of the Dharma. He also seems to be unaware of
my lecture 'The Individual and the World Today' (included in
New Currents in Western Buddhism), in which, having characterized the modern world as a Western world, a world which is
either Westernized or in process of Westernization, I continue:
'When I say that the FWBO is Western, I do not mean that it just
happens to be geographically located in the West, or that it was
started, geographically speaking, in the West; I mean that it has
arisen under the conditions of secularized and industrialized
Western civilization. And it is with those conditions that the

FWBO tries to cope. It tries to make the Buddhist way of life, the spiritual life ... possible, under these conditions. The FWBO is therefore Western in the sense that it is concerned with the world of today, not with the world of yesterday, however bright that world may have been in some respects. Nor is it primarily concerned with the world of traditional religious culture.... That world has gone, it seems, for ever.'[4] Mellor appears not to understand this. Indeed, though the FWBO is, according to him, 'a consciously "western" Buddhist group' (by the time we get to the second section of his article it has become 'self-consciously western') he makes no attempt to ascertain in what sense it is western and no attempt, therefore, to ascertain whether '"western" Buddhist group' and 'English Buddhist group' can really be treated as equivalent and the bearing this has on the 'complex relationship' of either or both of them (as the case might be) with 'Protestant Christian perspectives'.

The extent to which the FWBO is Western (in the non-geographical sense) varies from place to place. It is more Western in urban Germany than in rural India, for example, because the conditions with which it has to cope in the former are more secularized and industrialized than those with which it has to cope in the latter. Though in his introductory paragraph, as throughout his article, Mellor speaks of the FWBO as if it were a single, monolithic body this is not really the case. What we in fact have is an Order, members of which conduct, with the help of Mitras and Friends (as they are called), the activities of some fifty different FWBOs and other legally and financially autonomous bodies in more than a dozen countries both West and East. Like the Order itself, these FWBOs are united by a common spirit—a spirit which, in the case of the Order in particular, is symbolized by the figure of the eleven-headed, thousand-armed Avalokitesvara, the Bodhisattva of universal compassion. At the same time, each autonomous FWBO possesses its own distinctive character, a character in part determined by the extent to which it is (non-geographically) Western. In discussing the FWBO as 'a consciously "western" group' it is therefore not only necessary to understand in what sense it considers itself Western; it is also necessary to realize that it is not equally Western in all its parts.

But though the FWBO is not Western in the geographical sense, it of course started in the West. In started in London, the first of the autonomous FWBOs being founded there in 1967 and the WBO a year later. Autonomous FWBOs have since been established throughout Britain and in eleven other countries in four continents. At present (September 1991) there are in the world 450 men and women Order members (the WBO is a unified order in the sense that it admits men and women on equal terms), approximately 1,000 Mitras, more than a third of whom are postulants, and at a conservative estimate 100,000 Friends. Nearly twenty per-cent of all Order members are Indian, while there are twenty-one New Zealanders, thirteen Finns, and some two dozen representatives of fifteen or sixteen other nationalities. Among Mitras and Friends an even greater number of nationalities are represented, not to mention the imbalance created by the fact that the majority of Friends are Indian. Thus the FWBO is not English in the sense of having a purely English membership, and the extent to which it is English certainly varies from place to place. (Membership is by no means purely or uniformly English even in England.) The FWBO is English only in the sense that it started in England, and that the majority of Order members and Mitras are English—a state of affairs that on present form will not continue indefinitely.

Mellor is unaware of all this, just as he is unaware of the sense in which, and the extent to which, the FWBO is Western. For him the FWBO is simply a part of the English Buddhist scene and as such it is one of the two groups on which he proposes to concentrate his discussion of the relationship of contemporary English Buddhism with Protestant Christian perspectives, the other group being the English Sangha. The two groups are linked, he tells us, 'by the fact that neither are ethnic and that

Sangharakshita, the founder and leader of the FWBO, also led the English Sangha for a brief period in the 1960s before founding the FWBO.' By saying neither are ethnic Mellor appears to mean that both the FWBO and the English Sangha consist not of immigrant 'born Buddhists' but of native converts, which is correct (except that in the case of the FWBO the converts are not all English). Nonetheless there is an important difference between the two groups. The FWBO has always been self-sufficient, in the sense of depending for financial support on its own members rather than on the non-Buddhist and non-FWBO general public. This is one of the reasons for the existence of the various FWBO Right Livelihood businesses, which besides providing for the material and spiritual needs of their workers (who normally are FWBO members) donate their profits to one or more of the autonomous FWBOs. The English Sangha, on the contrary, is not self-sufficient, indeed cannot be self-sufficient. As a Theravadin (as distinct from, say, a Ch'an or Zen) monastic community it depends for support not on its own members but on the Buddhist and non-Buddhist general public. In practice this means that it depends largely, if not predominantly, on the support of the immigrant 'born Buddhist' laity, particularly as represented by the Thais, the English Sangha being closely related to the forest monasteries of Ajahn Chah in Thailand, as Mellor notes. The immigrant Thai laity support the English Sangha for the same reason, presumably, that they support monks in their own country. They support it in order to acquire 'merit' and to be reborn in heaven after death. Thus the English Sangha is brought within the orbit, to some extent, of Thai ethnic Buddhism. Merit is acquired by supporting monks, but only if the monks are 'real' monks, and what is a 'real' monk, that is to say, a monk of a holiness sufficient to guarantee that offerings made to him really are productive of 'merit', is in practice determined by the supporting laity, who are quick to withdraw their support from any monk failing to conform to their ideas of how a 'real' monk should behave. (Revealing light is thrown on the 'merit-making' side of Thai Buddhism in Timothy Ward's *What the Buddha Never Taught*, described as 'an open-eyed, often humorous, personal account' of the author's sojourn at Wat Pah Nanachat in north-eastern Thailand, one of the forest monasteries to which the English Sangha is closely related.[5]) To the extent that it is dependent on the support of the immigrant Thais, and within the orbit of Thai ethnic Buddhism, the English Sangha is inevitably under a certain amount of pressure to conform to its Thai supporters' idea of how a 'real' monk should behave and what is and what is not 'real' Buddhism. Even apart from other considerations, it is therefore doubtful if the English Sangha can be regarded as an English Buddhist group, and part of English Buddhism, without serious qualification.

The FWBO and the English Sangha are not only linked by the fact that, according to Mellor, 'neither are ethnic'. They are also linked by the fact that 'Sangharakshita, the founder and leader of the FWBO, also led the English Sangha for a brief period in the 1960s before founding the FWBO.' In fact I led it for two years, if indeed I can be said to have led a Sangha which for the greater part of that time consisted of only myself (the English Sangha is, of course, a Sangha of *monks*). These two years were among the most demanding and crucial—and the most spiritually rewarding—of my whole life, and I hope to be able to write an extended account of them one day. In the 1980s, however, Ajahn Sumedho, the present (American) leader of the English Sangha, was also for five years president of the Buddhist Society, founded in 1924 by Christmas Humphreys as the Buddhist Lodge of the Theosophical Society and the longest-established Buddhist organization in Britain. The English Sangha and the Buddhist Society thus are more 'linked' than are the English Sangha and the FWBO. I therefore wonder why Mellor concentrates his discussion on the relationship between 'contemporary English Buddhism' and 'Protestant Christian perspectives' on the FWBO and the English Sangha, rather than on the Buddhist Society and the English Sangha, especially as the Buddhist Society's activities are limited to England, not to say to the London area (except in the case of its journal *The Middle Way*, which circulates more widely). I also wonder why Mellor should be more concerned, apparently, with 'the markedly different visions of how Buddhism should be understood and practised in the west' demonstrated by the English Sangha and the FWBO than with whatever the two groups might have in common. In any case, if it is *differences* between English Buddhist groups which particularly interest him he ought to concentrate his discussion on the respective 'visions' of the English Sangha and the Buddhist Society, the 'vision' of the one being decidedly monastic in character and that of the other no less decidedly lay, as compared with the more unified 'vision' of the FWBO, which seeks to transcend the monk–lay dichotomy and to be simply and authentically Buddhist.

For reasons best known to himself, however, Mellor concentrates his discussion on the FWBO and the English Sangha, and it is in his discussion of the different approaches of these two groups that he draws his conclusions about 'the difficulties of translating an eastern religious tradition into a western cultural environment.' In responding to this discussion, and looking at the theoretical and methodological questions raised by Mellor's article, I shall not further concern myself with the ambiguities which, as I have shown, confront us in his introductory paragraph, even though the effect of these ambiguities is felt throughout much of the article. Nor shall I further concern myself with the English Sangha, except to the extent that misleading comparisons are made between it and the FWBO.

THIS SECTION of Mellor's article contains no direct reference to the FWBO or, for that matter, to any English Buddhist group. Its purpose seems to be to clear the ground prior to his engaging with the article's principal topic: the relationship between Protestantism, Modernism, and Culture, on the one hand, and Buddhism on the other. Mellor clears the ground by establishing, or seeking to establish, that in the contemporary West each person's self has become his principal burden; that this emphasis on self has diminished the significance of religious tradition; that one of the major defining characteristics of Buddhism is the rejection of self; and that the idea that a person's self is the principal burden has come to characterize certain areas of English Buddhism more than the traditional rejection of self. These positions have a definite bearing on what Mellor has to say about the FWBO in the discussion that follows, and I shall look at them carefully.

1 The idea that each person's self becomes his principal burden comes from Richard Sennett's *The Fall of Public Man*, an examination of the imbalance that exists between public and private life, its cause and significance. Mellor quotes the American sociologist as arguing that 'to know oneself has become an end, instead of a means through which one knows the world'.[6] This is corroborated, according to Mellor, by Edward Shils, who suggests that the attempt to discover oneself 'has come to be regarded as the first obligation of the individual',[7] an obligation that has meant that the significance of social ends has diminished and even called into question our ability to act, activity being only considered legitimate in as far as it takes place in an interpersonal context. Individuals withdraw into self, so Shils believes, 'to protect a precious psychic life which, it is understood, might wither if exposed to the harsh realities of the social world'.[8] Two causes which can be highlighted as being responsible for this emphasis on self are the Enlightenment (i.e. the eighteenth century philosophical movement of that name) and Protestantism. Shils in this connection 'notes the immense significance of the Enlightenment's concern for self-regulation and expression and the vision of the individual as a self-contained and self-determining moral entity,'[9] while Louis Dumont 'has drawn attention to the radical shift in significance from the Church to the individual in the doctrines of Luther and Calvin'.[10] Both the Enlightenment and the Reformation, in Dumont's opinion, have contributed to the modern view of the individual as a 'quasi-sacred absolute', so that transpersonal social forms (such as the Church) and even society itself are seen as insignificant, or even tyrannical.[11]

With much of this the (Western) Buddhist can agree, though the expression 'transpersonal' is ambiguous and needs to be examined. In the contemporary West there *is* an imbalance between public and private life, the attempt to discover oneself *has* come to be regarded as the first obligation of the individual, individuals *do* withdraw into self to protect a precious psychic life, and it is good that Sennett makes these things clear to us. *The Fall of Public Man* contains, in fact, a number of insights useful to anyone seeking to understand and practise Buddhism as this is understood and practised in the FWBO. Not that the idea of there being an imbalance between public and private life is really a new one, though Sennett certainly explores it more thoroughly than it has been explored before, or that the idea of one compensating for the other has not been expressed more clearly and more eloquently by earlier writers. In an article on 'The Isolation of Katherine Mansfield' John Middleton Murry comments on V.S. Pritchett's assumption that the cult of self-perfection is the natural compensation for the lack of a country in which one feels at home. 'Many have practised the cult of self-perfection, many indeed practise it today,' Murry writes, 'who have not been exiled from their native land. The natural consequence of living in exile from a familiar society is to seek compensation in a closer human relation. The friendliness, the ease of living, which is, as it were, diffused in one's manifold contacts with a familiar society, has to be recaptured in a more intense form in the ease and trust of more intimate and private relations. In a word, *the natural consequence of social insecurity is the search for security of love.'* [12]

This could hardly be better put. But the search for security of love (or the equivalent of love) is not confined to a single epoch or to any one quarter of the globe, any more than is the possibility of imbalance between public and private life. Even the idea of the self as a person's burden is to be found not only in the West but in the East, not only in twentieth century sociology and literary criticism but in ancient Indian philosophy and religion. It may surprise Mellor to know that the *Saṁyutta-Nikāya* or 'Book of the Kindred Sayings' contains a text called the *Bhārasutta* or 'Burden-sutta', in which the Buddha teaches the monks that the five khandhas, the five components of psycho-physical existence, are the burden, while the burden-taker (or burden-taking—the prose and verse portions of the sutta differ here) is the puggala, the individual, or person, or man, as the term is variously translated:

The burden is indeed the fivefold mass:
The seizer of the burden, man:
Taking it up is sorrow in this world:
  The laying of it down is bliss.

If a man lay this heavy burden down,
And take not any other burden up:
If he draw out that craving, root and all,
  No more an-hungered, he is free. [13]

Since it is one or another of the five khandhas, or the five khandhas collectively, that is wrongly imagined to be the 'self' (*attā, ātman*), for a person to have his self for a burden amounts to much the same thing as his having the khandhas for burden. Whether there really is a person (*puggala*) distinct from the khandhas was a matter of vigorous and prolonged debate between the different Buddhist schools from very early times, a debate which some would say in unconcluded even today.

However that may be, the circumstance that for the Buddha the self, or what is wrongly imagined to be the self, is a burden, albeit an existential rather than a purely psychological one, should be sufficient to alert us to the fact that to experience the self as burdensome is not necessarily a bad thing. Such an experience need not be the result of an imbalance between public and private life in the sociological sense, nor does it always have to be dealt with by trying to correct that imbalance on its own level. Moreover, the 'radical shift in significance from the Church to the individual in the doctrines of Luther and Calvin' to which, Mellor tells us, Louis Dumont has drawn attention, is not really of the same order as Shils's 'emphasis on self' and does not, therefore, support Sennett's argument about each person's self being his principal burden in the way Mellor implies. Taking our own look at Dumont's essay 'A modified view of our origins: the Christian beginnings of modern individualism', we find that for Dumont Calvin (and Luther to the extent that Luther's views are presupposed by Calvin) represents '*inworldly* individualism' and that this is compared with the '*outworldly* individualism' which characterizes early Christianity and the Indian world-rejecting religions including Buddhism. The experience of the self as burdensome again is hardly seen as a bad thing.[14]

2 For Mellor, however, the experience of the self as burdensome is definitely a bad thing. It is a bad thing because it 'produces' the fragmentation of society and the fragmentation of society

(Sennett's major concern, according to Mellor) means that the significance of religious tradition is diminished. The reason for this diminishment is that religious tradition 'is by its very nature something transpersonal' and what is transpersonal is, apparently, incompatible with modern individualism. At this point Mellor again refers to Shils, who 'notes the tension created between tradition and this emphasis on self' and whom he quotes as saying with regard to this emphasis: 'There is a belief, corresponding to a feeling, that within each human being there is an individuality, lying in potentiality, which seeks an occasion for realization but is held in the toils of the rules, beliefs and roles society imposes.'[15] Nor is that all. The acceptance of transpersonal norms is not only understood as unhelpful, Mellor explains, it is an encumbrance, for, according to Shils: 'To be "true to oneself" means ... discovering what is contained in the uncontaminated self, the self which has been freed from the encumbrance of accumulated knowledge, norms, and ideals handed down by previous generations.'[16] To commit oneself to a tradition means, on the contrary, placing limits on one's individual potential, a belief that is not unrelated, so Mellor assures us, to Luther's position in the faith or works controversy, 'itself an indicator of the shift of significance attached to the individual which Dumont has referred to.'

Not for the first time in this section of Mellor's article I find myself wishing that he would state his views in a plain and straightforward manner, instead of presenting them by means of references to, and quotations from, his various sociologist mentors. It would then be easier for us to see what he is getting at. But no doubt this sheltering behind 'authorities' is an accepted part of what is known as methodology, and *de rigueur* for a young academic. I shall therefore have to disentangle Mellor's views on the significance of religious tradition, and its alleged diminishment by individualism, as best I can, separating what is true in them from what is false and, in the process, making clear my own position on certain issues. Let me take for my point of departure the notion, attributed by Shils to those whose emphasis is on self, of 'the uncontaminated self, the self which has been freed from the encumbrance of accumulated knowledge, norms, and ideals handed down by previous generations.'

To me the idea that there exists a self which is pure, that this self is enslaved by socially imposed beliefs and customs, and that all one has to do in order to 'be oneself' and realize one's potentiality is to break free from them, is simply false. It is what I sometimes call Rousseauism, or pseudo-Rousseauism, in the sense of a popular version of the French writer's belief in the natural goodness of man, who he felt was warped by society. Such Rousseauism, I hold, has done a great deal of harm. It has encouraged people whose self was far from pure to give untrammelled expression to that self, thereby damaging themselves, other people, and society at large. It has encouraged the mistaken idea that institutions and rules are bad *per se*. It has encouraged an attitude of soul-destroying bitterness and resentment on the part of those who, having been brought up to think that the world owed them not just a living but ideal happiness, find themselves far from happy. It has encouraged the shifting of moral responsibility for one's actions from self to society. It has encouraged talk of rights rather than duties. Above all, perhaps, it has encouraged people to believe that they do not need to *work on themselves* but have only to change the social, economic, and political conditions under which they live. Such Rousseauism has nothing in common with Buddhism.

Nonetheless, the fact that no pure self exists on the mundane level envisaged by profane sociology and psychology does not mean that at the very apex of his being man does not possess (or rather, is not possessed by) a transcendental element of which he is normally unconscious. It is with reference to this element that the Buddha declares, in the *Aṅguttara-Nikāya* or 'Book of the Numerical Sayings', 'Luminous is this thought [or mind, or consciousness: *citta*], but it is defiled by adventitious defilements.'[17] Similarly, in the *Ratnagotravibhāga* it is said:

The element of Tathagatahood, as it is present in all, is immutable,
   and cannot be affected by either defilement or purification.
Like the Buddha in a faded lotus flower, like honey covered by a
   swarm of bees,
Like the kernel of a fruit in the husk, like gold within impurities,
Like a treasure hidden in the soil, like fruit in a small seed,
An image of the Jina in tattered garments,
The universal monarch in the vile belly of a woman,
And like a precious statue covered with dust,
So is this element established in beings
Who are covered with the stains of adventitious defilements.[18]

Here the thought is defiled by adventitious defilements, the element of Tathagatahood covered by the stains of those defilements. In order to reveal the inherent luminosity of the thought, to uncover the element of Tathagatahood, it is therefore necessary to get rid of the defilements, and it is with the getting rid of mental defilements that Buddhist praxis is, on its negative side, very largely concerned.

This does not mean that Buddhism is indifferent to social, economic, and political conditions, or that it disapproves on principle of trying to change them. There are some social, economic, and political conditions that are definitely unfavourable to the individual's efforts to rid himself of mental defilements, and it is entirely in keeping with the spirit of Buddhism that one should seek to replace these with conditions that are favourable to such efforts, though this must always be done by means that are in accordance with the spiritual end for the sake of which the change is made. Like those whose emphasis is on the self and who believe, according to Shils, 'that within each human being there is an individuality ... held in the toils of the rules, beliefs and roles society imposes',[19] Buddhism thus is prepared to countenance social reform, not to say social revolution, even at the risk of Sennett's 'fragmentation of society'. In the case of Buddhism, as represented for example by the ideal of the Dharmaraja, the 'Righteous Monarch' or 'Religious King', social reform is not countenanced in the interests of modern individualism, much less still in the interests of what I have called Rousseauism. It is countenanced in the interests of the individual-in-relation-to-Buddhahood (as we may describe him, adapting the terminology of Dumont's mentor Ernst Troeltsch), in order that his efforts to get rid of mental defilements may be facilitated and in order that, having rid himself of those defilements, he may reveal the inherent luminosity of thought, uncover the element of Tathagatahood, and achieve liberation not just from society, good or bad, but from mundane existence itself.

Here I must make two points. Firstly, the idea that there exists, on the mundane level, a self that is pure or 'uncontaminated', is not simply an idea that happens to be false; it is also one of the mental defilements and, as such, to be got rid of by the Buddhist or individual-in-relation-to-Buddhahood as quickly as possible. Moreover, notwithstanding loose talk in pseudo-Zen circles about oneself being in reality Buddha and having 'only' to realize the fact, it should be understood that the luminous thought, or element of Tathagatahood, is not to be regarded as lying as a potentiality within the mundane self in such a manner that the latter remains essentially unchanged even when that potentiality has been realized. In other words, realized or unrealized, the luminous thought, or element of Tathagatahood, is not to be regarded as a predicate of which the mundane self—Shils's 'individual as a "quasi-sacred absolute"'—is the perduring subject. Secondly, the conditions that are unfavourable to the individual's efforts to rid himself of mental defilements, and that therefore have to be changed, are not always social, or economic, or political in the narrower sense. The creation of conditions more favourable to the eradication of mental defilements, as well as to the cultivation of the positive counterparts of those defilements, may involve the repudiation of 'transpersonal social forms (such as the Church)'. It may even involve the rejection of religious tradition. This brings me back to Mellor and to his contention that religious tradition 'is by its very nature something transpersonal', what is transpersonal being, apparently, incompatible with modern individualism.

The term transpersonal is, however, an ambiguous one, and Mellor's use of it in this connection only serves to obscure a fundamental confusion in his thinking. That the term should be ambiguous is not surprising. It is not to be found either in *Collins* or the *Concise Oxford*, and seems to be a piece of undefined sociological jargon that Mellor has taken over from Dumont and Shils. The prefix *trans-* has four or five different meanings, only two of which are relevant here: it can mean 'beyond' in the sense of 'on the other side', and it can mean 'surpassing, transcending'. Thus 'transpersonal' can mean 'beyond the person', in the sense of 'on the other side of the person', and it can also mean 'surpassing the person' or 'transcending the person'—two very different things. I therefore suggest that when speaking of something as transpersonal in the first sense we speak of it as *horizontally* transpersonal, in the sense of its being beyond the person on the same level, and that when speaking of something as transpersonal in the second sense we speak of it as *vertically* transpersonal, in the sense of its being on a higher level than the person or occupying a different dimension. The distinction is an important one. Neither social forms nor religious traditions are necessarily transpersonal in the vertical sense, and the fact that Mellor does not realize this means that he is unable to see that the repudiation of social norms, and the rejection of religious tradition, is not necessarily an expression of modern individualism. He is unable to see that social norms and religious traditions may be transpersonal only in the horizontal sense, and that to repudiate and reject them may, therefore, be the act of the individual-in-relation-to-Buddhahood.

We thus have three possible scenarios: (a) Modern individualism versus the horizontally transpersonal, (b) modern individualism versus the vertically transpersonal, and (c) the individual-in-relation-to-Buddhahood—or, to speak in more general terms, the true individual—versus the horizontally transpersonal. (A fourth scenario, that of the individual-in-relation-to-Buddhahood versus the vertically transpersonal, is only a formal possibility, not a real one, involving as it does a contradiction in terms.) What Mellor in effect does is to treat all cases of scenario (c) as cases of scenario (b), and he is able to do this because he assumes, as Dumont appears to assume, that 'transpersonal social forms (such as the Church)' are necessarily transpersonal in the vertical sense, as is religious tradition. To understand the acceptance of transpersonal norms as not only unhelpful but an encumbrance therefore cannot but be a bad thing. Not to commit oneself to a tradition because this means placing limits on one's individual potential cannot but be a bad thing. The diminishment of tradition cannot but be a bad thing. The fragmentation of society cannot but be a bad thing. The experience of the self as burdensome cannot but be a bad thing.

In all this I detect the presence of a hidden agenda, the heads of which seem to be that society, i.e. Western society, must at all costs be held together, that it can be held together only by social forms (such as the Church) and (Catholic?) tradition, and that any attempt to undermine or diminish these must be discredited.

3 Though Mellor equates 'discovering what is contained in the uncontaminated self' with the diminishment of the significance of religious tradition, and this with the fragmentation of society which is produced by the modern burden of self, he is not afraid of a little inconsistency and is able to see self-discovery as not altogether a bad thing. Many notable religious figures, he tells us, have been sensitive to both the value and the dangers of self-discovery. St Theresa (of Avila), for example, affirms the value of self-knowledge at all levels of spiritual development, though using the metaphor of the bee (which must leave the beehive in order to gather nectar) she cautions against excessive self-absorption. 'The Buddha, however, is attributed with a far more severe rejection of self.' What St Theresa means by self-knowledge, and whether he considers her 'self-absorption' to pertain to the same order of experience as the 'self' rejected by the Buddha, Mellor does not say. Not that it really matters. St Theresa and her bee are introduced, apparently, simply as providing a means of transition to the Buddha and the 'far more severe rejection of self' with which he is attributed. 'He expressed the idea that it is because of the belief in self (*attā*) that people are vulnerable to the process of ageing, decay and dying, and therefore to suffering (*dukkha*).' This is all right so far as it goes, though it is by no means adequate as an account of the Buddha's teaching on the subject. Some Buddhists indeed would think it one-sided, especially as Mellor goes on to cite a contemporary Buddhist scholar's view that 'Buddhism aims at the salvation of the individual through the elimination of suffering, a process which necessitates the deconstruction of self, breaking down what appears to be "personal experience" into its constituent, *impersonal* elements.'[20]

This comes perilously close to saying that Buddhism seeks to save the individual by destroying him, a statement which though true in a certain paradoxical sense is not to be taken literally. Taken literally it amounts to the wrong, one-sided view of annihilationism (*ucchedadiṭṭhi*). What has to be destroyed is the wrong view that one or another of the five khandhas, or the five khandhas collectively, are the self or person, and whether after the destruction of that wrong view there was anything of the individual left was, like the larger question of whether there really is a person (*puggala*) distinct from the khandhas, a matter of debate. In the Buddha's case it was clear that, as he himself tells Anuradha in the *Saṁyutta-Nikāya*, it is not proper to say of him that he exists after death, or does not exist after death, or both exists and does not exist after death, or neither exists nor does not exist after death. None of these alternatives applies to him because 'in this very life a Tathagata is not to be regarded as existing in truth, in reality.'[21] Similarly, explaining to Ananda why he had remained silent when asked by the Wanderer Vacchagotta if the self exists, and again when asked if it does not exist, the Buddha says:

'If, when I was asked "Does self exist?" I had answered "Self exists," that would have been the belief of those who hold the theory of eternalism. And if, when I was asked "Does self not exist?" I had answered "Self does not exist," that would have been the belief of those who hold the theory of annihilationism. And if, when asked "Does self exist?" I had answered "Self exists," would that have been in conformity with my knowledge that all things are not-self? And if, when asked "Does self not exist?" I had answered "Self does not exist," then confused as he already is, Ananda, the Wanderer Vacchagotta would have become still more confused, assuming "Surely then I had a self before and now I have none."'[22]

The Buddha's attitude is pragmatic. It is better for Vacchagotta to go on believing he has a self, a belief which at least constitutes a basis for moral effort, than to believe that he has no self. Later it was sometimes said of the Buddha that he teaches annihilationists that the self exists, eternalists that it does not exist, and his own true followers that it neither exists nor does not exist.

But there is no need for me to pursue the subject. Mellor is not interested in the Buddha's rejection of self for its own sake. He is interested in it, as he goes on to show, only as a means of establishing that in respect of what he describes, not incorrectly, as one of the major defining characteristics of Buddhism, 'certain areas of English Buddhism' are not so much traditional as untraditional. In other words Mellor is interested in the Buddha's rejection of self as a stick with which to beat the FWBO.

4 He begins by blandly asserting that in view of the Buddha's rejection of self, the contemporary attachment to self which Sennett, Shils, and Dumont see as characteristic of the modern West ought to rule out the appeal of Buddhism in England (i.e. the appeal of Buddhism, in England, not the appeal of Buddhism-in-England). Previously he has quoted his sociologist mentors as speaking in terms of the *burden* of self, of the *discovery* of self, and of *emphasis* on self. He now represents them as all speaking in terms of *attachment* to self, which is not quite the same thing but which provides him with a sharper antithesis to that rejection of self which he has just described as one of the major defining characteristics of Buddhism. As I have shown, however, the experience of the self as burdensome is not necessarily a bad thing, so that the appeal of Buddhism in England need not be ruled out in view of the Buddha's rejection of self. Mellor switches to 'attachment' at this point simply as a means of emphasizing the unlikelihood of Buddhism appealing in England and to pave the way for his contention that some English Buddhists have adopted it for reasons connected with the un-Buddhistic idea that a person's self is their principal burden. Having asserted that the contemporary attachment to self ought to rule out the appeal of Buddhism in England, he therefore continues, with apparent candour: 'This is not so; neither is it generally the case that it has been adopted by a small group of people rebelling against this contemporary emphasis on self, though this is clearly true in some instances. Buddhism has had a much more sophisticated interaction with English culture.'

What this more sophisticated interaction is we shall see shortly. Just now it is important for us to take a closer look at how people in Britain actually come to 'adopt' Buddhism. From the fact that for him the contemporary attachment to self ought to rule out the appeal of Buddhism in England, and that he would have expected it, apparently, to be adopted generally by people rebelling against the contemporary emphasis on self, it is clear that Mellor tends to see the appeal of Buddhism in predominantly intellectual terms. Academic that he is, he sees people as adopting Buddhism for a single clear-cut reason, whether because it rejects self or whether because, as mistakenly supposed by those for whom the self is their principal burden, it does not reject self. But this is not really the case. On the basis of more than a quarter of a century's continuous experience of British Buddhism, I can assert that people adopt Buddhism for many different reasons and in many different ways, not all of them rational, and not all of them very direct or very clear. Some adopt it for intellectual reasons, some for emotional reasons, and some for practical reasons. Some adopt it because they want to deepen their experience of meditation, others because they are attracted by the personality of a particular Buddhist teacher, and yet others because they like the atmosphere of a particular Buddhist centre or group. Some even adopt it as a result of reading a book by Lobsang Rampa, or after seeing a Bruce Lee film. There are even people who adopt Buddhism because they are drawn by the Buddha's rejection of self, like the young woman, a university student, who once came on an early FWBO retreat. Whether she was a rebel against the contemporary emphasis on self I cannot say, but in the course of the retreat she told me that she had always been attracted by the anattā doctrine and that she had just realized why she was attracted by it. She was attracted by it because she hated herself and liked to think that she did not really exist.

People in fact adopt Buddhism (which is not necessarily the same thing as Going for Refuge to the Three Jewels) for a hundred different reasons, from the sublime to the silly and from the simplest to the most complex. Perhaps the commonest reason for their adopting it is that they are dissatisfied with themselves, or with life, or even that, in Karl Jaspers's phrase, they 'feel ill and suffer from their psychic state'. This does not mean that they are consciously 'attached' to self in Mellor's sense, that is, attached to it in a way that in view of the Buddha's rejection of self rules out the appeal of Buddhism. What it means is that they experience a sensation of lack, of there being something missing, and that out of this sensation they go searching, with varying degrees of determination and clarity, for that missing something, or at least are on the lookout for it from time to time. Not that they necessarily know what they are searching for, or have much idea where it is to be found; quite often they do not think of it as being 'religious' in nature at all, much less that it could possibly be connected with an 'eastern' religion like Buddhism. But sooner or later, in one way or other, such people come in contact with Buddhism, and having come in contact with it they feel, sometimes immediately, that the missing something has been found and that the sensation of lack is no longer there. This is, of course, only the beginning. Though what was missing has been found, the finders still have to take possession of it, or rather, have to allow it to take possession of them, a process which besides being a lengthy one entails painful conflicts between the mundane and the spiritual, attachment to self and rejection of self.

Mellor understands nothing of all this. Having singled out rejection of self as one of the major defining characteristics of Buddhism, he sees the religion as having been adopted, in England, by two different groups of people. There are those who are rebelling against the contemporary emphasis on self and there are those who are not rebelling against it, the latter apparently being very much in the majority. Thus it is that, according to Mellor, 'the idea that a person's self is their principal burden has come to characterize certain areas of English Buddhism more than the traditional rejection of self.' This is his 'more sophisticated' interaction of Buddhism with English culture, though presumably it is not so much the interaction itself which he regards as sophisticated as his own analysis of it. Not that he is unaware of the danger of over-stating his case. 'While it would be an over-exaggeration to assert that Buddhism in England can be understood exclusively as a participant in this personalizing trend,' he continues smoothly, 'it would also be misleading to avoid confronting the continuities between

English Buddhism and wider western trends, just because of our abstract perceptions of Buddhist doctrine.' Very true. But it would be no less misleading if on account of our abstract perceptions of Buddhist doctrine, and our ignorance of certain areas of English Buddhism, we were to imagine continuities where none really exist. Mellor concludes this section of his article with the statement: 'The religious and cultural context of English society must remain at the forefront of any study of the development of Buddhism in this country.' Indeed it must, except that one should not speak of the development of Buddhism in England as though it was synonymous with the development of Buddhism in Britain.

HAVING ESTABLISHED, to his own satisfaction, that the contemporary emphasis on self has diminished the significance of religious tradition, and that the idea that a person's self is his principal burden has come to characterize 'certain areas' of English Buddhism more than the traditional Buddhist rejection of self, Mellor is free to engage with his principal topic: the relationship between Protestantism, Modernism, and Culture, on the one hand, and Buddhism on the other. As we shall see, the Protestantism with which Mellor is concerned is, apparently, liberal Protestantism, and he approaches the relationship between Protestantism in this sense and English Buddhism via a brief consideration of the personalistic view of religion and the idea that there is a Buddhist 'essence' distinct from Eastern cultures. From liberal Protestantism it is, of course, only a short step to English Buddhism and to the question of why English Buddhists, when they criticize Christianity, direct their criticisms against Roman Catholicism rather than against Protestantism, and this in turn leads Mellor to his first direct comparison between the English Sangha and the FWBO—a comparison which involves, unfortunately, a serious misrepresentation of the FWBO's views in respect of several important issues.

1 'In the light of the cultural and philosophical trends affecting religion today,' Mellor declares, 'an effort should be made to stand apart from the view which characterizes religion in exclusively personalistic terms. We might take the view that religion is not, primarily, a private and personal matter.' Indeed we might, though Mellor does not particularize the cultural and philosophical trends affecting religion today, nor explain why an effort should be made to stand apart from the view which characterizes religion in exclusively personalistic terms. I myself take the view that religion is an *individual* matter, though I would not care to say that it was primarily an individual matter without first of all going into the question of what 'primary' means. Religion is an individual matter that has a subjective aspect, represented for instance by faith, prayer, and meditation, and an objective aspect, represented for instance by ethics, ritual, and myth. In Buddhist terms, the individual-in-relation-to-Buddhahood *subjectively* goes for Refuge to the Three Jewels and *objectively* manifests the Bodhichitta or (Cosmic) Will to En-lightenment, which latter is the other-regarding, altruistic dimension of the act of Going for Refuge and involves the prac-tice of the six (or ten) paramitās or 'perfections'. For me religion is both private and personal *and* objective and public because the individual himself is both subject and object, both soul and citizen, and I would not dream of characterizing it in purely per-sonalistic terms. So much is this the case, that normally I do not speak of the subjective aspect of religion as the private and per-sonal aspect, and have done so on this occasion only because Mellor does. For me the word private, especially as occurring in the phrase 'private and personal', has connotations of ex-clusivity and self-indulgence which render its use in connection with religion quite unacceptable. (Within the FWBO it was debated, a few years ago, whether Order members were entitled to a private life in the sense of one exempt from ethical scrutiny by their peers. There was general agreement that they were not.)

Nonetheless, Mellor seems to think that the FWBO does *not* stand apart from the view which characterizes religion in ex-clusively personalistic terms and that it takes the view that religion *is*, primarily, a private and personal matter. This quite gratuitous assumption serves to introduce what is, in fact, an astonishing *non sequitur*. 'The FWBO, for example [*sic!*], might *believe* that a Buddhist "essence" can be distilled from the east-ern cultures and traditions in which it has been located until the recent past, but we cannot accept this idea uncritically. We should note that this position demonstrates certain continuities with Protestant perspectives.' The FWBO's *belief* that there is a Buddhist essence is thus contrasted with the inability of Mellor and his sociologist friends to accept this idea uncritically. No attempt is made to ascertain the grounds of the FWBO's 'belief'. The contrasting of the two in this invidious fashion smacks, in fact, more of rhetoric than philosophy, and need be taken no more seriously than Mellor's assertion that the belief or idea that there is a Buddhist 'essence' demonstrates continuities with his now familiar 'Protestant perspectives'. All the same, whether accepted critically or uncritically, the idea that there is a Buddhist 'essence' is a crucial one, and I would like to offer a few common-sense observations on it before dealing with Mellor's remaining comments on the view that religion is essentially a personal, private matter.

The idea that there is an 'essence of Buddhism' is not a new one. Books have been written with this title, including a small but seminal one by D.T. Suzuki. The fact is, that however suspect it may be in the ultimate metaphysical sense, the idea that every existent thing has its own distinctive essence is a necessary presupposition of all discourse. Before we can discourse on a thing we must define it. Discourse *implies* definition. According to the dictionary, to define is to 'set forth [the] essence of' a thing (*Concise Oxford*), or '2. to describe the nature, properties, or essential qualities' of a thing (*Collins*). Thus when Mellor speaks of the rejection of self as 'one of the major defining characteristics of Buddhism,' he is in fact recognizing that Buddhism can be defined and, therefore, that it has an essence. Not that he is really disposed to question the idea that there is an 'essence of Buddhism'. All he wants to do, in this connection, is to make the point that unlike the credulous FWBO he is unable to accept the idea that Buddhism has an essence uncritically.

An essence is an essence of something. A Buddhist essence is the essence of 'Buddhist' culture and tradition, in which it is 'located'. Like the rejection of self, some elements in that culture and tradition may be major defining characteristics of Buddhism, and some may be minor defining characteristics. Other elements may not be *defining* characteristics at all, or may even be the contradictories of those characteristics. In other words, though a Buddhist essence is the essence of 'Buddhist' culture and tradition it is not necessarily present equally in all elements of that culture and tradition, and in the case of some elements may be entirely absent. The FWBO's belief that a Buddhist 'essence' can be distilled from the eastern cultures and traditions in which it has been located amounts to no more than the belief that it is possible to distinguish, within those cultures and traditions, between elements which are defining characteristics of Buddhism, whether major or minor, and those which are not. It amounts to the belief that it is possible to distinguish, within eastern 'Buddhist' cultures and traditions, between elements in which a Buddhist essence is present, to a greater or a lesser degree, and elements in which it is not present.

Mellor's inability to appreciate the grounds for the FWBO's 'belief' that there is an essence of Buddhism may not be unconnected with his failure to distinguish between Buddhism and the Dharma. He appears to be entirely unaware, throughout his article, that the modern Western term Buddhism is *not* interchangeable with the ancient Indian term Dharma or Dhamma and its Chinese and Tibetan equivalents, just as he appears to be unaware that the term religion cannot be applied to Buddhism uncritically or without reflection. In order to show the difference between 'Buddhism' and 'the Dharma' one has only to ask a question like, 'Is the practice of drinking alcohol an element of the Dharma/Buddhism?' Drinking alcohol is not an element of the Dharma because mindfulness, or recollection, is one of the defining characteristics of the Dharma and drinking alcohol is not conducive to mindfulness. In the drinking of alcohol the Dharma is not present (though some Vajrayanists would argue that it is). On the other hand, drinking alcohol may be an element of Buddhism in the sense of being an element in a certain 'Buddhist' culture and tradition, though it would be an element in which a Buddhist essence cannot be located. Thus there is a difference between 'Buddhism' and 'the Dharma', though the *essence* of Buddhism and the Dharma may be regarded as identical, the Dharma (-Vinaya) itself being described by the Buddha in teachings such as that given to Maha Pajapati, the Gotamid, in the Vinaya-Piṭaka or 'Book of the Discipline'.[23]

For Mellor Buddhism is, apparently, *all* the elements in 'Buddhist' cultures and traditions, whether a Buddhist essence is present in those elements or not. For him Buddhism is really no more than a culture. So successful is he in his own effort to stand apart from the view which characterizes religion in exclusively personalistic terms that, going to the other extreme, he ends up characterizing it in exclusively social terms. Having invited us to note that the FWBO's *belief* that a Buddhist 'essence' can be distilled from the eastern cultures and traditions in which it has been located, he therefore continues, invoking yet another of his mentors: 'As Jacob Neusner has pointed out, a major problem in the study of religion is that Protestant perspectives have combined with a post-Enlightenment scientific tradition to present religion as essentially a personal, private matter rather than an issue of culture.' From this he concludes: 'In studying contemporary religious change we are unlikely to be very sensitive to competing understandings of the nature of religion, or much else, if we share the same prejudices as one of our objects of study.' Which means, being interpreted, that the FWBO is prejudiced, because it takes the view that religion is, primarily, a private and personal matter! Mellor himself, of course, is free from prejudice.

2 A Christian scholar who has written extensively on Indian religions notes (as Mellor would say) that 'an elementary rule of methodology proscribes formulating a judgement on anything in categories foreign to it.'[24] The category Protestant is certainly foreign to Buddhism, yet despite having obtained his Ph.D. for a thesis dealing with problems of theory and method in the study of contemporary religion Mellor has no hesitation in describing certain characteristics that are significant factors in English Buddhism as Protestant characteristics. 'If we are to accept that certain Protestant characteristics are significant factors in English Buddhism,' he says, 'as I suggest we must, we are faced with the problem of knowing how to label this new religious form [i.e. English Buddhism] and the differentiations within it.' Not only does he formulate his judgement on English Buddhism in a category foreign to it; he 'suggests' that we *must* do this. True, he then asks: 'Is it legitimate to talk of Protestant Buddhism?' but like jesting Pilate he stays not for an answer, launching instead into a semi-critique of Ninian Smart's new 'pan-religious protestantism' to which I shall return. It would seem, however, that in some scholarly circles it *is* legitimate to talk of Protestant Buddhism. Chapter 6 of Gomrich and Obeyesekere's *Buddhism Transformed: Religious Change in Sri Lanka* is headed 'Protestant Buddhism', though here the Buddhism so categorized is not English Buddhism but the 'modernist' Buddhism of Sri Lanka which Anagarika Dharmapala is regarded as exemplifying. It is also legitimate, it would seem, to talk of Puritan Buddhism, and even of a Puritan Buddha, as John Stevens does in *Lust for Enlightenment: Buddhism and Sex.* Soon it will be legitimate to talk of Quaker Buddhism, Evangelical Buddhism, Anglican Buddhism, Primitive Methodist Buddhism, and Hard-shell Baptist Buddhism. For all I know, some scholars are doing this already.

But to return to Smart's 'new pan-religious protestantism'. Mellor is not altogether happy with this. We should be very dubious, he thinks, about the evolutionary framework of Smart's position, and about that position's implicit approval of a trend which is envisaged as sweeping away all the 'external organisation and rituals of religion', as well as unpalatable dogmas and doctrines. Nevertheless Mellor finds Smart's analysis of religious history useful. Among other things, in such an analysis 'it is possible to elucidate the specific character of English Buddhism in the light of an awareness of this liberal Protestant trend.' Thus from categorizing English Buddhism as Protestant he passes, without comment, to categorizing it as liberal Protestant. He also passes from describing 'significant factors' in English Buddhism to elucidating its 'specific character'. But though he makes no attempt to define Protestantism, he does at least describe liberal Protestantism, and for this small mercy we must be thankful. 'Some major characteristics of liberal Protestantism, in a Christian context,' he informs us, 'are an emphasis on faith above knowledge, on the individual person above the community, and on the rejection of doctrines such as the authority of the Church, the Virgin Birth, the Incarnation and even the existence of God.'

Liberal Protestantism thus is undeniably liberal. Indeed, I must admit that despite occasionally reading the religious affairs section of a leading daily I had not realized how far, in the case of Protestant Christianity, the process of liberalization had gone and how many traditional doctrines had been rejected; but Mellor has a Ph.D. in Theology and I suppose I shall have to take his word for it. Having told us the worst about liberal Protestantism, of the Christian variety, he goes on to claim that 'pan-religious protestantism' is, as Smart suggests, the product of such rejections of traditional Christian doctrine, 'questionings and increased emphases on the individual reaching an extreme level where they exceed the boundaries of what can legitimately be called Christianity. At this point "Buddhism" becomes a more attractive structure for individuals pursuing their spiritual goals.' Precisely as he had passed from Protestantism to liberal Protestantism, Mellor now passes from liberal Protestantism to pan-religious Protestantism, proposing in fact that *this* is the framework within which we might consider English Buddhism. Smart's analysis of the trend of religious history has a definite value for Mellor, even though he is critical of his demi-mentor's evolutionary narrative, but before we can see how that value becomes clear I want to refer back to his claim that it is at the point where the boundaries of what can legitimately be called Christianity are exceeded that 'Buddhism' becomes a more attractive structure for individuals pursuing their spiritual goals.

There is no doubt that there is such a thing as pan-religious Protestantism, and no doubt that it is at the point where the boundaries of traditional Christianity are exceeded that for some individuals in Britain 'Buddhism' becomes a more attractive structure. In the case of many of these individuals, however, Buddhism, or what they think of as Buddhism, is simply that: it is 'more attractive'. Though they might have rejected traditional Christian doctrines, or allowed them to slip away from them, they retain a sentimental attachment to Christianity which prevents them from committing themselves wholeheartedly to Buddhism or, in traditional Buddhist terms, from Going for Refuge to the Three Jewels. Thus they in fact remain within 'pan-religious Protestantism' or within what I sometimes call pseudo-universalism. What proportion of the membership of Buddhist groups in Britain (other than the FWBO) such individuals make up today I do not know, but in 1964 they were very much in the majority and it was partly for this reason that I eventually decided that a new, more authentically Buddhist movement was needed in this country.

3 The value of Smart's analysis of the trend of religious history becomes clear, according to Mellor, when one considers the degree to which English Buddhists, when the criticize or attack Christianity, appear to be thinking mainly of Roman Catholicism. The principal 'problems' attributed to Christianity by English Buddhists are, in his view, authoritarianism, institutionalism, dogmatism, triumphalism, ritualism, and formalism, all of which are charges traditionally directed at Catholicism by Protestants, and it at first seems odd that English (or American) Buddhists, coming from a firmly Protestant culture, should direct their criticisms against a Catholic form of Christianity. 'Surely,' he objects, 'if western Buddhists were keen to differentiate themselves from their surrounding religious context, Protestantism should be the likely target?' It is only at first that it seems odd, however. Mellor is ready with an explanation. The fact that English (or American) Buddhists direct their criticisms against a Catholic form of Christianity, instead of at Protestantism, 'underlines the fact that western Buddhists and liberal Protestants have a great deal in common'. Not that he is suggesting that English Buddhism is not really Buddhism at all, Mellor hastens to assure us, but only that it is 'useful' to place it in a liberal Protestant trend, albeit one of a 'pan-religious' kind.

Whether the 'problems' attributed to Christianity by English Buddhists *are* all charges traditionally directed at Catholicism by Protestants it is not necessary to enquire. Nor is it necessary to enquire whether the culture from which such English (or American) Buddhists come is as 'firmly Protestant' as Mellor seems to think it is. The explanation of why the FWBO, at any rate, criticizes Roman Catholicism, and does not criticize Protestantism, is really quite simple, and has nothing to do with the 'fact' that western Buddhists and liberal Protestants have a great deal in common. But before giving that explanation I would like to express a wish.

In Parliament there is a practice known as 'declaring an interest'. If an honourable or right honourable member happens to have a connection, especially a prejudicial connection, with the matter under debate, he makes this known. I wish there was a similar practice within the academic community. I wish scholars would declare an interest when they have a personal connection, perhaps one that is of great emotional importance to them, with the subject that is being discussed, instead of writing or speaking as though their attitude was one of complete scientific objectivity and impartiality. Philip Mellor, I am told, is a Roman Catholic, in fact a convert to Roman Catholicism, and he as such has a personal connection with criticisms of Roman

Catholicism on the part of English Buddhists. But he does not make this known, he does not declare an interest, with the result that his approach to such criticisms, like his approach to English Buddhism, in particular to the FWBO, perforce is oblique and tangential, not to say covert, tempting uncharitable English Buddhists who have not forgotten their Bible to exclaim, with the dying Isaac, 'The voice is Jacob's voice, but the hands are the hands of Esau.' I therefore put it to Mellor that if he again writes on English Buddhism he should write as a believing and practising Roman Catholic rather than as an amateur sociologist. He has nothing to lose by so doing, at least in FWBO eyes. Personally, I would much rather he quoted Augustine and Aquinas at me than Sennett, Shils and Co. It would be more of an honour to be proved wrong by him with *their* help than to prove him wrong despite the support given him by his sociologist mentors. But enough of quixotry! I have expressed my wish. Now let me give my explanation.

The reason the FWBO criticizes Roman Catholicism, and does not criticize Protestantism, is not only quite simple; it is one which reflects no discredit on Roman Catholicism. Since the tenth century, the time of the *filoque* dispute, Roman Catholicism or Latin Christianity as we may also call it, has been the normative form of the Christian faith in Western Europe. It is Roman Catholicism that for nearly a thousand years dominated our social, political, artistic, and intellectual life and even today, if we look at the west front of Chartres Cathedral, or read Dante, or visit the Arena Chapel, or listen to Palestrina or Monteverdi, it is Roman Catholicism that we encounter. When Western Buddhists criticize or attack Christianity it is therefore of Roman Catholicism that they are mainly thinking, this being the form of Christianity with which they are, historically speaking, most familiar. They generally are not thinking of Protestantism, which may be described as Roman Catholicism in dilution. Protestantism may also be described, changing the metaphor, as the rebel child of Roman Catholicism, or rather as a whole tribe of rebel children (and grandchildren) who, as well as rebelling against their venerable Mother, until quite recently were often at logger-heads among themselves. Western Buddhists therefore usually do not care to criticize Anglicanism or Lutherism, Pres-byterianism or Methodism, or any of the other forms of Western Christianity, except perhaps on points wherein they differ from Roman Catholicism as well as from Buddhism itself. If they criticize Christianity at all they criticize Roman Catholicism, for in criticizing Roman Catholicism they are, in principle, criticiz-ing them all.

But there is another reason why the FWBO, at least, does not criticize Protestantism. I have described Protestantism as Roman Catholicism in dilution, but what is the diluting element? The diluting element is secular humanism, by which I mean (a) the theory or doctrine that concerns itself with man rather than with something other than man, and concerns itself with him, moreover, as possessing no transcendental (*lokuttara*) dimen-sion, as well as (b) the attitude and the practical consequences that go with such a theory or doctrine. Rousseauism, or pseudo-Rousseauism, with its belief in the natural goodness of man and the warping effect of society, is a form of secular humanism, and as I have already made clear it has nothing in common with Buddhism. Criticisms which Mellor seems to think should be directed against Protestantism are in effect directed, in the case of the FWBO, against the secular humanist element in Protestan-tism. They are not directed against Protestantism as such be-cause there is, in a sense, no such thing as Protestantism. There is only Roman Catholicism and secular humanism: (Catholic) Christianity and materialism—both of which Western Buddhists have, by definition, repudiated.

4 Though for Mellor both the English Sangha and the FWBO have a relationship to liberal Protestantism there are, he believes, differences between them in terms of that relationship. In fact he is concerned to emphasize that this is the case.

Unfortunately, his discussion of these differences, besides being bedevilled by his insistence on placing the FWBO within a liberal Protestant trend, is confused by his penchant for labelling the English Sangha and the FWBO as more or less 'self-conscious', or more or less 'sophisticated', the one than the other, in this or that respect. Ignoring these irrelevancies, I shall concentrate on the way in which he compares the two groups with regard to selectivity in respect of Buddhist doctrine and practice, making Buddhism accord with Protestant sensibilities, the issue of morality, and the issue of ritual observances.

Whereas the FWBO, according to Mellor, is 'manifestly selective in which elements of Buddhist doctrine and practice it chooses to accept' the English Sangha 'locates itself in the Thai forest tradition'. This is rather disingenuous. One could just as easily say that the English Sangha is manifestly selective in which elements of Thai Buddhist doctrine and practice it chooses to accept and that the FWBO locates itself in the ecumenical Buddhist tradition as represented, for example, by the Chinese T'ien-t'ai School and the nineteenth century Tibetan Ri-me movement (to which several of my own teachers belonged). The fact is that Western Buddhism, or Western Buddhists, cannot but be selective, in that Buddhism is so vast in extent and so rich and varied in content that there can be no question of literally accepting it *in toto*. One is *forced* to choose. The only question is that of the basis on which the selection, or choice, is made. Broadly speaking, there are two possibilities: one can select an existing eastern Buddhist tradition, i.e. join it and follow it on its own terms, or one can select doctrinal and practical elements from one or more eastern Buddhist traditions and synthesize them in such a way as to create a 'new' Buddhist tradition. The English Sangha follows the first course. From among the different schools of Buddhism it has chosen the Theravada (not the T'ien-t'ai, the Hua-yen, the Gelugpa, the Nyingmapa, the Zen, the Shin, etc.), from among the different forms of the Theravada it has chosen the Thai (not the Sinhalese,

the Burmese, the Cambodian, or the Laotian), and from among
the different Thai traditions it has chosen the forest tradition
(not the city tradition). The FWBO follows the second course.
While in principle it accepts Buddhism *in toto*, practically speaking it selects doctrinal and practical elements mainly from the
Theravada, the Mādhyamika-Yogācāra, the T'ien-t'ai, the
Nyingmapa, and the Ch'an/Zen schools.

In this connection there are two points to be borne in mind.
Firstly, in selecting doctrinal and practical elements from one or
more eastern Buddhist tradition the FWBO is doing no more, in
principle, than individual eastern Buddhists, or groups of eastern Buddhists, do in the case of their own particular tradition. A
Sinhalese Theravada monk, for example, while in principle accepting the Theravada tradition *in toto*, will not familiarize himself with *all* the doctrines, including those of the Abhidhamma,
nor will he practise *all* the forty methods of meditation
(*kammaṭṭhāna*) described in the *Visuddhimagga*. He will *select*. He
will study, perhaps, the *Dhammapada* and the *Sutta-nipāta* and
practise the mindfulness of in-and-out-breathing (*ānāpānasati*).
Secondly, the FWBO has been in existence for nearly twenty-five
years and there is now an FWBO tradition. Individuals in Britain
(and elsewhere) for whom Buddhism has become, in Mellor's
phrase, a more attractive structure, no longer have only eastern
Buddhist traditions to choose from. They have the possibility of
selecting a *Western* Buddhist tradition—a tradition in which the
Dharma is communicated in a way that directly addresses their
own situation and their own spiritual needs.

5 Speaking of the English Sangha's relationship to liberal Protestantism, Mellor makes the point that Ajahn Sumedho has often
referred to his own Protestant background, and has noted the
suspicion among visitors and the ordained at Amaravati of
things which are associated with Catholicism, such as rituals, incense, and chanting. Implicitly, according to Mellor, the Ajhan 'is
aware that Buddhism in the west can, as he sees it, be deformed

through the desire to make it accord with Protestant sensibilities. On the other hand, there is no evidence of any leading figure in the FWBO publicly worrying about Protestant characteristics which may exist in the FWBO, despite the extreme and open contempt persistently directed towards (Catholic) Christianity. This seems to signify a marked difference in the two forms of Buddhism.' Once again we have the 'Protestants under the bed' syndrome. There is no doubt that among visitors and Friends at FWBO centres in Britain, as among visitors and the ordained at Amaravati, there is suspicion of things Catholic; but this is at least as likely to be due, I have found, to a painful experience of Roman Catholicism as to a Protestant (actually secular humanist) cultural conditioning. Leading figures in the FWBO do not worry, publicly or otherwise, about Protestant characteristics which may exist in the FWBO because, as I have explained, there is in a sense no such thing as Protestantism and because Buddhism in the West can, as they see it, most easily be deformed through the desire to make it accord with Rousseauistic, secular humanist, or pseudo-liberal sensibilities.

Whether the English Sangha is quite so free from this latter desire as Mellor seems to think, I do not know. At any rate, I remember one of my Theravadin correspondents telling me, shortly before my return to Britain in 1964, that the Hampstead Buddhist Vihara was so located because Hampstead was where the left-wing intellectuals lived and these were the people who were most likely to be interested in Buddhism. I should add that during the two years that I led the English Sangha, and lived at the Hampstead Buddhist Vihara, I did not to my knowledge see there a single 'Hampstead intellectual'.

6 Another difference between the English Sangha and the FWBO, according to Mellor, is in their approach to doctrine and traditional practices. The FWBO, he says, has a very liberal approach: 'whatever does not assist "individual development" must be discarded, as Subhuti asserts.' (Here a note refers us to

Buddhism for Today, p.35, but in fact there is no mention of individual development on that page of Subhuti's book, or indeed in that chapter. 'Check your sources,' was a famous old scholar's dying advice to a young disciple who wanted to know the secret of his success.) Once again Mellor is being disingenuous. Provided individual development is understood, as the FWBO understands it, as development in the direction of Enlightenment (*bodhi*), one could just as easily say that the FWBO has a very *traditional* approach to Buddhist doctrine and Buddhist traditional practices. After all, no Buddhist school would be prepared to maintain, as a matter of principle, that doctrines and traditional practices that did not assist individual development should *not* be discarded, though there might be disagreement as to whether certain doctrines and practices were unhelpful or not. Even the English Sangha would not be prepared to maintain *that*! The fact is, Mellor is far too ready to see differences between the English Sangha and the FWBO. Not that there are not differences: there are; but there are similarities too. After observing that the English Sangha, despite its strictness in following the doctrines and rituals of the Thai forest tradition, often talks of 'etiquette' rather than rules, and stresses the self-discovery of truth rather than the doctrinal definition of it, Mellor goes on to describe Ajahn Sumedho's problems with the issue of morality. When the Amaravati community was established in 1977, the Ajahn found that morality was associated with being narrow-minded, 'pre-modern', and that to talk about it was 'driving people away', so that he had to assert that 'Buddhist moral precepts are standards to be reflected on' rather than something imposed or used in a judgemental way. 'Hence, he modified his presentation of Buddhist morality but still asserted its significance although lay people did not want to hear about it at all: "They wanted to hear about having more and more freedom to develop themselves."'

This was very much my own experience at the Hampstead Buddhist Vihara in 1964, as well as during the early years of the

FWBO. I too found that for many people the word morality had a distinctively negative connotation, so that like Ajahn Sumedho thirteen years later I had to assert that Buddhist moral precepts were standards to be reflected on. In my case, however, this involved no modification of my presentation of Buddhist morality, since I had always presented it in this way and was to continue to do so. As I wrote in *The Ten Pillars of Buddhism*: 'What the Ten Precepts really represent are principles of ethics, or ethical principles. They are not rules, in the narrow, pettifogging sense of the term ... though rules may be founded on them, or derived from them. If we could think of the Precepts as being what in fact they are, ethical principles in accordance with which, as a result of our commitment to the Ideal of Enlightenment, we are doing our best to live, a good deal of this confusion would be avoided. We would also find the Precepts themselves more inspiring.'[25] These words were originally addressed to members of the Western Buddhist Order, the work from which they are taken having first seen the light of day as a paper read to Order members in 1984, on the occasion of the Order's sixteenth anniversary. Ajahn Sumedho's words, taken from a public talk given at Amaravati two years later, were spoken with reference to lay people, as distinct from monks. It was lay people who did not want to hear about morality at all, lay people who wanted to hear about having more and more freedom to develop themselves, and lay people, presumably, for whose sake he was obliged to modify his presentation of Buddhist morality. In his case the difficulty may have been due partly to the nature of the Theravada, for which there exists a world of difference between monks and lay people and for whom the monk is the real Buddhist. It is the monk who leads the spiritual life, the monk who practises meditation, the monk who observes the 227 precepts of the Vinaya or Monastic Code, the lay people being little more than his humble supporters. Hence Theravada lay people, more often than not, do not feel themselves sufficiently Buddhist to take a serious interest in morality. In the West they may not even want to hear about it and may want, instead, to hear about having more and more freedom to develop themselves.

Interestingly enough, it is immediately after quoting Ajahn Sumedho's complaint about lay people wanting to hear about having more and more freedom to develop themselves that Mellor refers to the FWBO as having, 'on the other hand', a very liberal approach to doctrine and traditional practices: 'whatever does not assist "individual development" must be discarded, as Subhuti asserts.' The fact that the two quotations are juxtaposed in this way suggests that the 'freedom to develop themselves' of which Ajahn Sumedho complains and Subhuti's 'individual development' are more or less the same thing. But really they are very different things. The freedom about which Ajahn Sumedho's lay people want to hear is, presumably, the freedom of modern individualism, whereas the development of which Subhuti speaks is the development of the individual-in-relation-to-Buddhahood or true individual. Mellor has again confused two scenarios and, by seeking to equate something upheld by Subhuti with something complained of by Ajahn Sumedho, not only misrepresents the FWBO but exaggerates the differences between the FWBO and the English Sangha. Still more interestingly, perhaps, by one of those *non sequiturs* of which he is almost as fond as he is of the labels 'self-conscious' and 'sophisticated', Mellor jumps from his quotation from Subhuti straight to an assertion about the FWBO's approach to religious truth: 'The FWBO manifests an exclusivist approach to religious truth: not only are the theistic religions objects of harsh criticism, being associated with "authoritarianism, dogmatism, fanaticism, inhumanity, weakness and guilt", but other forms of Buddhism are labelled "middle-class", "dilettante" exoticism.' Subhuti's reasoned criticism of the theistic religions (Mellor is again quoting from *Buddhism for Today*) though admittedly harsh is fully in accordance with Buddhist tradition, as a glance at Helmuth von Glasenapp's *Buddhism—a Non-Theistic Religion*, for example, will amply demonstrate. I shall therefore say no more of Mellor's assertion that the FWBO manifests an exclusivist approach to religious truth, especially as he follows it up with yet another *non sequitur*, to the effect that in relation to a general cultural 'concern for questions of selfhood' (Sennett), the FWBO does not find itself at odds with contemporary western culture but firmly in line with it.

I would, however, like to comment on two of his references to the English Sangha. Having pointed out that, for the English Sangha, the Thai forest tradition is an absolute standard by which the tradition in England must be judged, so that discipline, hierarchy, doctrine, and ritual observances are followed as strictly as possible in the West, Mellor observes, 'On the other hand, it often talks of "etiquette" rather than rules.' If it really does this the English Sangha is much more 'liberal' than the FWBO. There is, of course, a section of the Vinaya that is concerned with what are, in fact, only matters of etiquette (not that etiquette is unimportant), but to talk of etiquette *rather* than rules is, in traditional Buddhist terms, to reduce pakatisīla or natural morality to pannatisīla or conventional morality and, in effect, to deny the significance of morality altogether. Similarly, having described Ajahn Sumedho's discovery that morality was associated with being narrow-minded, and so on, Mellor observes, 'He had to assert that "Buddhist moral precepts are standards to be reflected on" rather than something imposed or used in a judgemental way.' The word judgemental is not in the *Concise Oxford Dictionary* (though it is in *Collins*), and I hope Ajahn Sumedho himself did not use it, since it is a piece of pseudo-liberal jargon the connotations of which are anything but Buddhistic. 'Oh one mustn't be judgemental!' cry those of the pseudo-liberal persuasion whenever an attempt is made to apply ethical principles to specific instances of human behaviour. This amounts to denying that there is such a thing as ethics or any objective values.

7 Yet another (alleged) difference between the English Sangha and the FWBO is in respect of ritual observances. According to Mellor, the issue of ritual observance is 'a major point of divergence' between the two forms of English Buddhism. The FWBO, he says, is highly suspicious of ritual and has shorn Buddhism of what it understands to be the unnecessary and cluttering baggage of eastern cultural accretions. Here a note refers us to *Buddhism for Today*, p.6, but in fact there is *absolutely no mention* of ritual observances on this page and *absolutely no mention* of unnecessary and cluttering baggage, whether that of eastern cultural accretions or anything else. But to proceed. Having declared the FWBO to be highly suspicious of ritual, and 'quoted' Subhuti in this connection, Mellor continues: 'It has developed certain rituals and ceremonies of its own, however, though form is understood to be strictly subordinate to a personalistic content, and practices such as making offerings to monks and prostrating oneself before them are firmly rejected.' Here a note refers us to *The History of My Going for Refuge*, pp.74–5. But what do I actually say there? After referring to the fact that during my stay at the Hampstead Buddhist Vihara I had read a book on the Second Vatican Council in which the Roman Catholic Church was said to be characterized by triumphalism, I described how there suddenly struck me, with the force of a thunderbolt, the thought that the Theravada monastic order, too, was characterized by triumphalism.

'I recalled occasions on which Sinhalese monks had arrogantly insisted on taking precedence of everyone else and on being treated, in effect, like VIPs, in the belief that they were thereby upholding the supremacy of the Dharma. Similarly, I recalled the way in which visiting Thai bhikshus had confined themselves to teaching the newly converted ex-Untouchable Buddhists such things as how to prostrate themselves before members of the monastic order and how to make offerings to them, as though in so doing they were propagating Buddhism among the ex-Untouchables with a vengeance....

'Strange to say, at about the same time that I became aware that the Theravada monastic order was characterized by triumphalism I became more aware of the fact that there was a good deal of triumphalism in my immediate surroundings, as well as a good deal of formalism. Four or five Sinhalese and Thai monks were then staying with me at the Hampstead Buddhist Vihara, and all of them manifested a degree of triumphalism in their dealings with British Buddhists. So much was this the case, indeed, that I was reminded of the way in which the visiting Thai monks had taught the ex-Untouchable Buddhists, for though the monks who were staying with me at the Vihara certainly did not confine themselves to teaching their British disciples how to prostrate themselves before members of the monastic order and how to make offerings to them there was the same disproportionate emphasis on these things that I had witnessed in India.'

Thus there is no question of practices such as making offerings to monks and prostrating oneself before them being 'firmly rejected', as Mellor alleges. What I reject in this passage is the *disproportionate emphasis* on these things that is characteristic of south-east Asian bhikkhus. Nor is that all. Mellor speaks of the FWBO as 'firmly rejecting' (ritual) practices *such as* making offerings to monks and prostrating oneself before them, thereby clearly implying that there are (ritual) practices *other than* these that are rejected by the FWBO and of which I make mention in the passage in question, whereas this is not the case. In the same devious manner, immediately after asserting that the FWBO is 'highly suspicious of ritual', he observes, 'The English Sangha encourages ritual activity such as chanting, bowing, the use of candles and incense, and the offering of *dana* gifts along with the all-embracing disciplinary structure legitimated with reference to tradition,' thus suggesting that these ritual activities are *not* encouraged by the FWBO.

It is difficult to know where Mellor got his impression, indeed his conviction, that the FWBO is 'highly suspicious of ritual', since he certainly did not get it from the sources to which he refers, and it is difficult to know just how to go about exposing the extent of his misrepresentation. Perhaps I had best begin by investigating whether the ritual activities encouraged by the English Sangha are encouraged by the FWBO or not, and then comment on Mellor's more general observations on the FWBO's attitude to ritual.

Chanting is practised throughout the FWBO, including FWBO centres and communities in Britain, and is an integral part of its religious life. In the case of the Refuges and Precepts chanting is in Pali, in the case of mantras in Sanskrit. Sometimes devotional verses are chanted in Tibetan. Bowing is a hardly less popular ritual practice, the value of which is well understood. As Tejananda writes, after explaining the significance of the añjali-salutation or salutation with joined fingertips:

'Salutation, bowing, and prostration may be made at any appropriate moment when one feels moved to do so, but especially upon entering or leaving a shrine room, and when making a personal offering of flowers, lights, or incense at the shrine. Often, when making offerings, people make a more complete oblation to the Buddha by kneeling and lowering the forehead to the ground, at the Buddha's feet, so to speak. An even more complete salutation is the full prostration—throwing the entire length of one's body onto the ground in front of the shrine. These practices have a tremendous effect in reducing one's tendency to pride and egotism, as well as enhancing one's receptivity to the Ideal.'[26]

In *Buddhism for Today* there is a chapter on 'Bowing Before the Buddha' which Mellor appears to have overlooked, and which contains, incidentally, a description of recitation and chanting as practised in the FWBO. It was on account of this and another chapter that Gerald du Pré, the chairperson of the Scientific Buddhist Association, on the appearance of Subhuti's book in 1983, criticized the FWBO for being under the necessity of emphasizing spiritual friendship and puja or ritual worship because it was not sufficiently scientific to be able to function without them. Prostration, in the sense of the Tibetan Buddhist Going for Refuge and Prostration Practice, is the principal subject-matter of chapter 11 of *The History of My Going for Refuge*, entitled 'More Light from Tibetan Buddhism', in the course of which I refer to the fact that some members of the Western Buddhist Order had completed the 100,000 repetitions of the ('Tantric') Refuge-going formula and 100,000 prostrations of this particular mūlayoga or foundation yoga. In this connection I recall an early convention of the Order on which I opened the shrine room door one afternoon to be confronted by the inspiring spectacle of some three dozen perspiring men and women Order members totally absorbed in doing the very strenuous Going for Refuge and Prostration Practice together. It is strange that a Buddhist group that is highly suspicious of ritual should encourage salutation, bowing, and prostration in this way, but Mellor says the FWBO is highly suspicious of ritual, and Mellor has a Ph.D. in the problems of theory and method in the study of contemporary religion.

Candles and incense are widely used in the FWBO. Together with flowers, also widely used, these constitute the three basic ritual offerings made to the Buddha-image in all forms of Buddhism. As Subhuti puts it:

'They are expressions of the gratitude which it is natural to feel to those who have given the Dharma. When one receives something, one will feel grateful and want to give something oneself—not by way of exchange but spontaneously, in appreciation. Like bowing, the making of offerings in this way provides an opportunity to express gratitude and devotion and to cultivate these feelings if one does not readily experience them. During [FWBO] ceremonies there is often a point at which those principally concerned, for instance individuals being ordained, make offerings, and in daily devotional ceremonies everyone can go forward to light incense at the shrine. The consequence of such actions should be experienced in other aspects of life: one will feel more generous and thankful in all one's relationships, particularly with those who are, in any sense, one's teachers.'[27]

Nor is it only candles, incense, and flowers that are used in the FWBO. Besides the seven 'external offerings' of Indo-Tibetan Buddhism, such things as mandala-type cosmographs, miniature Pure Lands, and models of the Seven Jewels of a World Conqueror may also be ritually offered to the Buddha-image. On the occasion of ordinations and Mitra ceremonies, new Order members or Mitras, as the case may be, offer gifts to their teachers and themselves receive gifts from friends and well-wishers. I particularly recall a women's ordination retreat some years ago on which, having conducted the ordinations and received my own offerings, I sat watching with great pleasure the pile of gifts in front of each new Dharmacharini steadily growing as, one by one, the seventy or eighty other women present on the occasion came forward and offered each Dharmacharini in turn a card, a bunch of flowers, a poem, or a book. Again it is strange that a Buddhist group that is highly suspicious of ritual should encourage the use of candles, incense, flowers, and other ritual items, as well as the offering of dana gifts, in this way, but Mellor says the FWBO is highly suspicious of ritual, and Mellor has a Ph.D. in the problems of theory and method in the study of contemporary religion.

Mention could also be made of the fact that the FWBO's first publication was *The FWBO Puja Book*, which has now sold well over 15,000 copies.[28] In her introduction to the fifth (Windhorse) edition Dhammadinna writes:

> 'Poetry, symbol, myth, and ritual carry us, as Shelley sug-
> gests in his *Defence of Poetry*, "to regions of light and fire,
> where the winged faculty of calculation dare not ever soar".
> We cannot live in the realm of rational thought alone. To feel
> fully and vibrantly alive, we must feel in touch with all the
> different aspects and levels of our being.
>
> 'Buddhism is a spiritual tradition, and as such speaks to us
> in our wholeness. Its various practices can help us to bring
> into being a harmony of body, speech, and mind.
> Throughout its history, therefore, many forms of ceremony
> and ritual have been developed.'[29]

Whereas the *Puja Book* consists of texts for recitation and chanting, and as such is of a practical nature, another FWBO publication is concerned with the theory and rationale of ritual. This is
Puja and the Transformation of the Heart, two essays by Tejananda
and Vessantara which in their Mitrata and Windhorse editions
have sold altogether 8,000 copies. Tejananda's essay, 'Faith,
Devotion and Ritual', from which I have already quoted, not
only explains the purpose of ritual and devotion in Buddhism,
and specifically the purpose of practices of this sort used in the
FWBO, but also surveys some of the reasons why Westerners, in
particular, so frequently experience adverse reactions to these
practices. Yet again it is strange that a Buddhist group that is
highly suspicious of ritual should seek to promote recitation and
chanting, and to explain the purpose of Buddhist ritual and
devotion, in this way, but Mellor says the FWBO is highly suspicious of ritual, and Mellor has a Ph.D. in the problems of theory
and method in the study of contemporary religion.

But the FWBO is not only highly suspicious of ritual, has not
only shorn Buddhism of what it understands to be the unnecessary and cluttering baggage of eastern cultural accretions. As we
have already seen, according to Mellor 'It has developed certain

rituals and ceremonies of its own, however, though form is understood to be strictly subordinate to a personalistic content,
and practices such as making offerings to monks and prostrating oneself before them are firmly rejected,'—and it is to these
more general observations and the FWBO's attitude to ritual that
I must now go back. I have already pointed out that what I actually reject in the passage in *The History of My Going for Refuge*
to which Mellor's note here refers us is the *disproportionate emphasis* on making offerings to monks and prostrating oneself
before them that is characteristic of south-east Asian bhikkhus,
indeed of south-east Asian Buddhism. Hence it will not be
necessary for me to consider the question of making offerings to
monks and prostrating oneself before them on its own merits, so
to speak, though I would like to observe that monks who have
become accustomed to the prostrations of 'lay people' can easily
develop an inflated idea of their own spiritual attainments. The
questions I shall consider relate to whether the FWBO has
developed rituals and ceremonies 'of its own', and whether
form is, in fact, understood to be 'strictly subordinate to a personalistic content'.

In conceding that the FWBO, despite its suspicion of ritual, has
developed rituals and ceremonies 'of its own', Mellor seems to
be conjuring up a picture of an essentially 'Protestant' Buddhist
movement reluctantly devising observances that have no basis
in tradition. This is far from being the case, as the merest glance
at *Puja and the Transformation of the Heart* and *The FWBO Puja Book*
would have sufficed to show him. The Tiratana Vandana or
'Salutation to the Three Jewels', the Going for Refuge and
Taking of Precepts, the Short Puja, and the Sevenfold Puja, all of
which figure prominently in the devotional and ritual life of the
FWBO, are thoroughly traditional in character. Even the Dedication Ceremony, which I composed for the opening of the Trirat-
na Shrine and Meditation Centre in 1966, draws on traditional
material. Indeed, the production of liturgies for the use of one's
disciples is a traditional Buddhist activity, as witness the

enormous number of such liturgies in the canonical Buddhist languages—liturgies that were certainly not all produced by the Buddha in the fifth or sixth century BCE. During the last three or four years, moreover, a group of Order members has been engaged in trying out 'new' rituals and ceremonies with a view to their eventual introduction into the mainstream of the Movement. Like my own Dedication Ceremony, these rituals and ceremonies draw on traditional material and are as much, or as little, the FWBO's 'own' as the rituals and ceremonies of Sinhalese Theravada, for example, or of Japanese Soto Zen, are *their* own.

Whatever the nature of the FWBO's rituals and ceremonies, it certainly is not true to say with regard to them that form is understood to be strictly subordinate to a personalistic content, and I am at a loss to know what could have led Mellor to make such a statement, especially as the reference he gives in this connection is to the passage in *The History of My Going for Refuge* in which I allegedly reject 'practices such as making offerings to monks and prostrating oneself before them'—a passage in which, moreover, there is no mention of 'form' and no mention of any 'personalistic content'. Not for the first time, Mellor attributes to the FWBO views that are the exact opposite of those it actually holds and has, in this case, always held. For the FWBO, form is *not* subordinate to a personalistic content. In my lecture 'The Psychology of Ritual', given in 1968 and the source of much of the FWBO's thinking on the subject, I speak of (rational, as distinct from neurotic) ritual in terms that are anything but personalistic. Following Erich Fromm, I define it as *shared* action, expressive of *common* strivings rooted in *common* values, the implication being that the performance of ritual is possible only within a spiritual community or, as one might also say, within *vertically* transpersonal social forms and religious traditions.

But the question of form—or rather of rejection of form—is one that seems to bother Mellor. Having stressed the English

Sangha's encouragement of chanting, bowing, and so on, and duly noted the tension introduced into these practices because of the association of ritual with Catholicism, he observes that owing to the religious background of England ritual is necessarily a more self-conscious form of activity, if not a problematic one, than it is in Thailand, and that this difficulty is increased when 'the Protestant suspicion of ritual becomes reinforced by a strong emphasis on the Buddhist rejection of form; that is, the distinction between two levels of truth, the provisional (or the conventional) and the ultimate, where it is understood that even "Buddhism" as a form can be discarded.' This is perfectly true, and after commenting that caution about the use of ritual and form in the West can be inspired by factors other than the Buddhist doctrine of ultimate truth, and quoting Steven Collins to the effect that the Buddhist denial of self appears only in certain contexts, at a highly sophisticated level of doctrine, and that the use of the term 'self', or other categories of the person, appears throughout other levels of doctrine, Mellor rightly remarks: 'An awareness of such sophistication in traditional Buddhist discourse is important because it enables us to be cautious about a tendency in some areas of western Buddhism to forget about "provisional" truth altogether.' Whether the FWBO is to be understood as being (wrongly) included in the areas of Western Buddhism referred to is unclear, but presumably it is, especially as Mellor has somehow become convinced that the FWBO is highly suspicious of ritual and might, therefore, be expected to reject form and forget about provisional truth no less readily than it subordinates its 'own' rituals and ceremonies to a personalistic content. Be that as it may, his remark serves to bring Mellor back to the English Sangha and to Ajahn Sumedho's understanding of religious form. According to Mellor, though the Ajahn understands religious form as ultimately 'empty', and 'not an end in itself', he still asserts the value of secondary, conditioned forms, and Mellor goes on to quote him as saying:

'Some modern day religious leaders tend to say: "Don't have anything to do with religious convention. They're all like the walls of prison cells"—and they seem to think that maybe the way is to just get rid of the key. Now if you're already outside the cell of course you don't need the key. But if you're still inside then it does help a bit.'

The religious leaders of whom Ajahn Sumedho is thinking are probably Krishnamurti and Rajneesh, latterly known as Osho. Mellor, in all likelihood, is also thinking of Sangharakshita—and of the FWBO. But if this is the case I shall have to disappoint him. As should be obvious from what I have already said about the FWBO's alleged suspicion of ritual, I am in complete agreement with Ajahn Sumedho on this point, though since he is so very much my junior it might be more in accordance with tradition to say that he is in agreement with me. I too, unlike some modern day religious leaders, assert the value of secondary, conditioned forms, and assert it strongly, even though understanding religious form to be ultimately empty and not an end in itself. For me, as for Ajahn Sumedho (according to Mellor), 'the Buddha did not make a distinction between provisional and ultimate truth in order to make provisional truth appear valueless.' The only respect in which I differ from Ajahn Sumedho is that for me the fact that one 'needs the key if one is still inside the cell' is *not* a basis from which I can 'stress the value of *all* religious form, both within Buddhism and without it'. For me there is some 'religious' form, both within and without 'Buddhism', that is definitely not of value, that is, not of value to the individual who is seeking to develop in the direction of Enlightenment. To assert otherwise is to come dangerously close to pseudo-universalism and pseudo-liberalism.

Thus the issue of ritual observance is not nearly so much a point of divergence between the English Sangha and the FWBO as Mellor asserts. In principle there is probably no divergence between them at all on this score. Any divergence in practice is due, I suspect, to the FWBO's having a wider range of ritual activities than the English Sangha and conducting them, moreover, on a grander scale and in a more colourful manner. If Mellor would do a little field work, and attend (for instance) an FWBO Buddha Day celebration, he might be agreeably surprised. Admittedly he would not see much in the way of people making offerings to *monks* and prostrating themselves before them, but he would see Order members, Mitras, and Friends engaging in traditional Buddhist practices of many other kinds. So seeing, he might realize, not only that the FWBO is *not* 'highly suspicious' of ritual but that he had, perhaps, thought this to be the case because he somehow had been led to believe that making offerings to monks and prostrating oneself before them was the Buddhist ritual activity *par excellence* and that, without it, a Western Buddhist group could be safely assumed to reject ritual altogether.

But I am anticipating. Mellor is not quite finished with ritual and form. Having quoted Ajahn Sumedho to the effect that the Buddha did not make a distinction between provisional and ultimate truth in order to make provisional truth appear valueless, he concludes this section of his article by drawing attention—via a citation from R.J. Zwi Werblowsky, yet another of his sociologist mentors—to the fact that the form of Thai forest monasticism upon which the English Sangha is modelled is itself an extreme form which understands itself as a 'revival' of Buddhism, a response to the 'domesticated' Sangha of Thailand. 'The syncretism characteristic of so much south-east Asian Buddhism is rejected in the teaching of Ajahn Chah, as is a great deal of ritual associated with the "institutionalized" Sangha of the cities. The "simplicity" of Ajahn Chah's teaching is persistently emphasized and seen as one of its most attractive characteristics, especially to westerners.' The significance and value of ritual is not something which would automatically be endorsed by Ajahn Chah, who in fact instructs lay visitors not to 'get caught up with outward form', while still asserting the value of monastic rules and discipline. All this makes the Thai forest tradition sound quite 'Protestant' in character. Not that the English Sangha is necessarily equally 'Protestant'. As Mellor points out, in a Western context Ajahn Sumedho faces a very different problem, a major danger being not of people getting caught up in outward form, but them rejecting form altogether. To the fear of many English Buddhists that they might 'cling' too much to tradition, Ajahn Sumedho responds that 'One can also cling to the idea that one does not need tradition.' Once again I am in agreement with Ajahn Sumedho—or he with me.

Mellor comments that Ajahn Sumedho has brought the Thai forest monastic tradition to England without 'adapting' it, but has recognized that context will have its effect, and that the tradition 'would take its own form accordingly'. Similarly, in a passage from my interview with Mellor—a passage that I have already quoted and to which, as I then said, Mellor makes no reference—I explain that on my return to Britain 'I was just concerned to teach the Dharma, not any Western version of it.... I'm not trying to "adapt" the Dharma; I'm just trying to make it understandable. If one can talk of a Western Buddhism [at all] it is only in the sense of a form in which the Dharma can be understood and practised in modern Western society. [So far as I am concerned] it is not an "interpretation" of the Dharma.' In other words I, like Ajahn Sumedho, 'envisage a form [of Buddhism] that is traditional yet sensitive to its local context', though in my case that form is perhaps envisaged on a more generous scale and in relation to a broader context.

FROM PROTESTANTISM to modernism is but a small step. Another of Mellor's mentors, the Catholic theologian Hans Urs von Balthasar, 'has noted the genealogical link between liberal Protestantism and the phenomenon of modernism', and modernist narratives, so Mellor informs us, 'have been instrumental in the development of some contemporary, or recent, religious perspectives'. Since he views the FWBO as demonstrating 'continuities with Protestant perspectives' and as being, therefore, a form of 'Protestant Buddhism', it is not surprising that Mellor should view the FWBO as demonstrating continuities with modernist perspectives too. Half way through his discussion of modernism and Buddhism he in fact throws his customary caution to the winds and roundly declares 'The FWBO is modernist.'

Modernism is (a) the comprehensive term for an international tendency arising in the poetry, fiction, drama, music, painting, architecture, and other arts of the West in the last years of the nineteenth century and subsequently affecting the character of most twentieth century art; and (b) in theology, the movement to modernize doctrine by taking into account the results of higher criticism and scientific discovery, and the conditions of modern culture, but chiefly the term used as a label for the outlook of a group of Roman Catholic thinkers led by Alfred Loisy and George Tyrrell. But it is not modernism in the artistic sense, or even in the narrowly theological sense, that Mellor really has in mind in this section of his article, despite the fact that he speaks of (theological) modernism as having been condemned by the Roman Catholic Church. For him the modernist perspective, as he prefers to term it, 'is one which coerces historical phenomena into an evolutionary, singular narrative where the modern constantly supersedes, and therefore makes irrelevant, the traditional and the orthodox'. This perspective 'can happily co-exist with liberal Protestantism which also rejects the traditional and the orthodox, in terms of both dogma and religious practice, in favour of an increasingly personalist understanding of religion.' In other words, modernism is for Mellor the belief that the new is by definition better than the old, especially as that belief finds expression in the sphere of religion. Admittedly Mellor does not actually speak of the modern as being, for modernism, 'better' than the old. He speaks of it as *superseding* the traditional and the orthodox and making them *irrelevant*— fashionable, non-evaluative terms I would not have expected to find a man of his sympathies using. But from the whole trend of his discussion it is evident that for him modernism is, in fact, the (false) belief that the new is by definition better than the old, especially as that belief finds expression in the sphere of religion.

Now let me say at once that I do *not* believe that the new is by definition better than the old, whether in the arts or in religion, and at no time in my life have I been tempted to believe this to be the case. Thus I am not a modernist, at least not in the sense in which Mellor uses the term, and the FWBO is no more modernist than it is Protestant. For me Bertrand Russell is not necessarily a greater philosopher than Plato, nor Francis Bacon a finer painter than Botticelli. Priority and posteriority of achievement have nothing to do with relative merits. This is not to deny that *Hamlet* is superior to *Gorbuduc*; it is simply to affirm that *Hamlet* is superior *and* later, not superior *because* later. But not only do I not believe that the new is by definition better than the old. If I may be permitted to sound a confessional note, I actually love the old more than the new and have always done so. In literature, in the visual arts, and in architecture, as well as in philosophy and religion, I have always loved the pre-modern (classical, medieval, and Renaissance) much more than the modern, and have sometimes wished that I lived in an earlier period of history. Once I remarked, not altogether in jest, that I had a thoroughly medieval cast of mind, by which I meant that for me it was natural to think in terms of hierarchy and degree. (Nowadays, of course, 'medieval' is often assumed to be synonymous with 'primitive' and 'backward' and, therefore, with 'bad'. Prison conditions, for example, are said to be medieval.) Thinking in terms of hierarchy and degree as I do, it is not surprising that my views on many current social issues should not only be at variance with pseudo-liberalism but should be regarded, in some quarters, as positively reactionary.

That I love the old more than the new is not, of course, necessarily supportive of my belief that the new is *not* by definition better than the old. I mention my love for the old simply in order to show that I am not only not a modernist but have no disposition towards modernism. Mellor is able to label the FWBO as modernist simply because he has not bothered to find out what my views, or the views of the FWBO, really are, and he has not bothered to find out because, having proved to his own satisfaction that the FWBO is 'Protestant', he assumes that, there being a 'genealogical link between liberal Protestantism and the phenomenon of modernism', the FWBO is necessarily modernist. This specious logic enables him to misrepresent and misinterpret the FWBO's position on a variety of topics, from the relation between Buddhism and evolution to the necessity of ethics, and from the nature and value of tradition to the significance of 'charismatic authority', and to some of the more serious of these misrepresentations and misinterpretations I must now turn. Before turning to them, however, I would like to make some additional comments in connection with (a) (theological) modernism and (b) the new.

(a) 'The Roman Catholic Church condemned modernism at the turn of the century,' Mellor informs us, 'but within certain Protestant groups it has flourished.' This is rather disingenuous, suggesting as it does that Pius X had the last word on the subject and that the phenomenon was thereafter unknown within the

Petrine communion. (Theological) modernism represented, among other things, an attempt to take into account the results of higher criticism and scientific discovery, and while it would be an exaggeration to claim that modernism has ever flourished within the Catholic Church, even in the wake of Vatican II, there is no doubt that some of the results of higher criticism have been quietly appropriated by Catholic scholars and theologians. One of the consequences of this at a popular level has been the removal from the Calendar of Saints of the names of Catherine (of Alexandria), Christopher, and Ursula, on the grounds that they were probably non-existent, even though tradition had long held them to be historical personages. The same type of development is illustrated by an amusing episode in Giuseppe di Lampedusa's novel *The Leopard*, when a priest who had been a pupil at the Vatican School of Palaeography spends three hours examining the seventy-four holy relics which three aristocratic old spinster sisters have collected over the years and pronounces *five* of them authentic. All the other little bits of bone and gristle could be thrown on the rubbish heap; they had no value whatsoever.

The fact is that all religions are having to take into account, and if possible come to terms with, the results of higher criticism and scientific discovery, and this inevitably sets up tensions and conflicts within their respective structures. Buddhism is no exception. I well remember the storm that, in the Ceylon of the fifties, broke on the devoted head of the Director of Archaeology, himself a Theravada Buddhist, when he suggested that the Buddha had *not* personally visited the island three times. That he should be dismissed from his post was the least of the punishments demanded by his 'orthodox' co-religionists. I myself, at about the same time, shocked a Sinhalese Buddhist woman who was on pilgrimage in India by appearing to doubt that the Buddha was eighteen feet tall. 'What sort of monk is *this*?' her expression very clearly conveyed. But things appear to be changing, both in Theravadin Sri Lanka and in other parts of

the Buddhist world. The Dalai Lama, I hear, has recently written
to Tibetan monks engaged in propagating Buddhism informing
them that when in the West they did not have to teach that the
Earth is flat, even though this is what Tibetan Buddhist tradition
avers. Whether they were free to teach that the Earth is flat
when in the East was not made clear. Like that of the Buddha's
three visits to Sri Lanka, or that of his being eighteen feet tall,
the example is an obvious and even a ludicrous one, but its very
ludicrousness serves to underline the fact that we can ignore the
results of higher criticism and scientific discovery only at the
cost of our intellectual integrity—an integrity which is inseparable from moral and spiritual integrity. We can ignore
them only by retreating into an attitude of obscurantism.
Whether in Christianity or in Buddhism, (theological) modernism of a limited type would appear to be inescapable.

(b) In 1969 I wrote a poem entitled 'New', in which I wished I
might speak in a new voice, communicating new things and
celebrating 'The new horizon, the new vision/The new dawn,
the new day.' I quote this poem at the end of 'My Relation to the
Order', the paper I produced for the twenty-second anniversary
of the Western Buddhist Order. In case Mellor chances to see this
paper and accuses me of expressing, in the poem, sentiments at
variance with what I say above about my not believing the new
to be by definition better than the old I should like to explain
myself. 'New' is not necessarily the opposite of 'old'. It can also
indicate that which does not really belong to the temporal order
and which is, therefore, neither old nor new. Thus it is possible
to distinguish between the vertically new and the horizontally
new, as we may term them, the vertically new being that which
has no connection with time but which irrupts into, or manifests
within, the temporal process, from another dimension, while the
horizontally new is simply that which is unprecedented in time.
The vertically new may be signalized by an upper case initial
letter, leaving the horizontally new unsignalized in this way.
What is New may, of course, also be new, but it is not New

because it is new. It is New because it is New. When I wish, in my poem, that I might speak in a new voice, communicating new things and celebrating 'The new horizon, the new vision / The new dawn, the new day,' the new to which I refer is the New, not the new. Its affinities are not so much with the 'Make it new' of Ezra Pound as with the 'Behold, I make all things new' of the Apocalypse.

1 For Mellor, as we have seen, 'a modernist perspective is one which coerces historical phenomena into an evolutionary, singular narrative where the modern constantly supersedes, and therefore makes irrelevant, the traditional and the orthodox'. Whether or not this is the case, Mellor certainly tries to force the FWBO into a modernist perspective, i.e. into the general framework of modernism. 'The FWBO uses what are recognizably modernist narratives and appears to embrace enthusiastically the personalist understanding of religious significance which developed in liberal Protestantism. In fact, these two perspectives come together in Sangharakshita's assertion that Buddhism affirms "individual rather than collective values", corresponding to and coinciding with "the upper reaches of the total evolutionary process". Subhuti also talks of the "suprahistorical", "upward surge of the individual".' That the FWBO does *not* embrace 'the personalist understanding of religious significance', whether enthusiastically or otherwise, has already been made clear (*vide supra*, p.46 *et seq.*), so that there is no question of its sharing the modernist perspectives that 'relegate religion from a socially significant, institutional level to a private, personal sphere' and no question of its being, like liberal Protestantism, 'happier to see it there'. Still less is there any question of the FWBO sharing the point of view of Wilfred Cantwell Smith who, according to Mellor, argues that there is no such thing as 'religion', only 'a vital personal faith'.

Since the FWBO does not embrace liberal Protestantism's personalist understanding of religious significance it is difficult to see how the two perspectives, the personalist and the modernist, could 'come together in Sangharakshita's assertion that Buddhism affirms "individual rather than collective values", corresponding to and coinciding with "the upper reaches of the total evolutionary process".' The individual values to which I refer are not private and personal values; they are the values proper to (true) individuals *and* the spiritual community (i.e. the community of [true] individuals) as distinct from the values of group members and the group. The nature of the difference between the spiritual community and the group, and between group members and those who are (true) individuals, as well as the nature of the consciousness or awareness that characterizes the spiritual community as such, is discussed in the very section of the *History* from which Mellor purports to quote, as are the social or communal, higher-evolutionary, and cosmic contexts in which the individual's Going for Refuge takes place. This discussion Mellor completely ignores. He takes one phrase from the third page of this section, another from the fourth, reverses the order in which they occur in my text, and strings them together in a 'quotation' he then proceeds to treat as evidence of my holding views diametrically opposed to those I actually do hold. Thus he not only tries to force the FWBO into a modernist perspective; in order to accommodate my views within his own preconceived notions about the FWBO he goes so far as to truncate what I have written. Presumably this Procrustean procedure is what he understands by methodology.

Whether or not this is the case, Mellor's determination to see the FWBO as a form of 'Protestant Buddhism' and as demonstrating, therefore, continuities with both liberal Protestantism and modernism, is truly remarkable. What is the reason for this determination? Reluctant as I am to ascribe motives, in the absence of any objective grounds for his (distorted) perception of the FWBO I have no alternative but to assume that the grounds are subjective and that, whether he recognizes it or not, Mellor's attitude towards the FWBO is controlled by a hidden agenda of the type to which I referred in connection with his failure to distinguish between the horizontally transpersonal and the vertically transpersonal (*vide supra*, p.38). That this may well be so is indicated by the fact that his 'quotations' from Subhuti and myself are immediately succeeded by the complaint that, in this 'evolutionary structure' of ours, 'Christianity has played its part in the development of the individual (from a lower level of consciousness) but has now been superseded by the higher path of Buddhism.' There's the rub, it would seem. 'Christianity is now a danger to the individual who wants to develop. To support this view, the FWBO can use both modernist secularization narratives and liberal Protestant Christian complaints about Roman Catholicism. Both support the idea that the world is evolving in a particular direction which leaves traditional Christianity behind.' Let us see to what extent Mellor's complaint is justified and whether the FWBO does, in fact, use modernist secularization narratives and liberal Protestant Christian complaints about Roman Catholicism to support its (alleged) view that Christianity is a danger to the individual who wants to develop. But first a few words about the total evolutionary process, i.e. about the other of the two perspectives that according to Mellor come together in my assertion that 'Buddhism affirms "individual rather than collective values", corresponding to and coinciding with "the upper reaches of the total evolutionary process".'

The concept of evolution is a comparatively recent one which, having been successfully employed as a principle of explanation in biology, has been extended to cover practically all other branches of knowledge. In speaking of Buddhism in evolutionary terms I am not however equating Buddhism with evolutionism of the Teilhardian type; much less still am I claiming that the Buddha anticipated Darwin (I shall have something to say about Scientific Buddhism later on in this section). I am simply using the concept of evolution as a medium for the exposition of Buddhism. Such a procedure is, of course, double-edged. As Subhuti observes, the danger, here, is that old meanings may reassert themselves when an old language (in this case the language of biology) is made to express new (in this case Buddhist) understandings. 'Western Buddhists today often borrow the language of other systems—psychoanalysis, science, Christianity—but they underestimate the power which old meanings retain. Already some Buddhist groups seem more like psychotherapy gatherings, or those of humanists, or even of thinly disguised Christians. The importance of creating and safeguarding a new and diamond-clear vocabulary for the expression of the Dharma is obvious.'[30] The term 'evolution' can, I believe, be part of that vocabulary, the more especially since there is a degree of overlap between the principle of evolution and one of the fundamental principles of Buddhism, i.e. the principle of conditioned co-origination (*pratītya-samutpāda*). As I have explained elsewhere, Buddhism is a path (more correctly, the principial Path).

'In one form or another, the concept of the Path has always been central to Buddhism. The Path consists of steps or stages. These steps or stages represent, essentially, states of consciousness, or of being, which are progressive, leading the individual from ignorance to Enlightenment, from the condition of *pṛthagjana* to that of Arhant or Buddha. One could therefore say that the conception of spiritual development, or spiritual *evolution* (what I call the Higher Evolution of Man) is central to Buddhism.'[31]

Higher implies lower. That there is a Higher Evolution of Man means there must also be a Lower Evolution. For many years I was concerned only with the Higher Evolution, because I was concerned only with Buddhism, only with the Path taught by the Buddha. But eventually I came to realize that the principle of the Higher Evolution was reflected, in a distorted and fragmented manner, in the whole biological process from amoeba to man, and that this reflection was the Lower Evolution.

> 'Science revealed how far man had come. This was the Lower Evolution. Buddhism, as the Path, showed how far he still had to go. This was the Higher Evolution. Though not strictly continuous the two phases between them constituted the two halves of a single process.'[32]

There was, in fact, a qualitative difference between the two halves, for though both were governed by the same universal principle, the principle of conditioned co-origination, they were governed by two different modes of it, the cyclical and the spiral. The difference was exemplified within the Path itself, in the broadest sense, only the upper reaches of which constituted the Path proper or transcendental Path, the lower reaches being spiritually-positive but mundane. The crux of the difference between the two modes of conditionality was that in the former the reaction took place in a cyclical order between two opposites, such as pleasure and pain, virtue and vice, good and evil, while in the latter it took place in a progressive order between two counterparts or complements or between two things of the same genus, the succeeding factor augmenting the effect of the preceding one. Transition from the cyclical to the spiral mode of conditionality, from the lower reaches of the Path to the Path proper, constituted what was traditionally known as Stream-Entry. It was also known as the Point of No Return. Once past that point, one was no longer governed by the cyclical mode of conditionality, and could not react to any opposite. One could only go forward.

Prior to that point, however, one *could* react to an opposite; one could suffer a relapse, could decline, could deteriorate. Thus the whole biological process up to and including pre-Stream-Entrant man and his social, economic, political, and cultural history was characterized, not by continual progress but by progress interrupted by regress and regress by progress, with the ever present possibility of total relapse, total decline, and total deterioration. Continual progress was possible only on the transcendental Path. Only in the case of the steps or stages of the transcendental Path was the new invariably, and necessarily, better than the old. Only on the transcendental Path was the new always the New. If a modernist perspective is one which, in Mellor's words, 'coerces historical phenomena into an evolutionary, singular narrative where the modern constantly supersedes, and therefore makes irrelevant, the traditional and the orthodox,' then it follows that there can be no question of the FWBO using 'recognizably modernist narratives', and no question of modernist and personalist perspectives ever coming together in any statement of mine. For the FWBO, as for the rest of the Buddhist world, the evolutionary narrative is not singular but dual, the total 'evolutionary' process comprising as it does a Higher Evolution governed by the spiral trend of conditionality and a Lower Evolution governed by the cyclical trend. As for Subhuti's 'supra-historical', 'upward surge of the individual', this represents the emergence of the spiral process within the cyclical, the manifestation of the transcendental within the mundane, and no more represents a 'recognizably modernist' narrative than do my own words.

2 In Sangharakshita's and Subhuti's evolutionary structure, Mellor complains, 'Christianity has played its part in the development of the individual (from a lower level of consciousness), but has now been superseded by the higher path of Buddhism. Christianity is now a danger to the individual who wants to develop.' Had the FWBO shared the modernist perspective, and had it really coerced historical phenomena into 'an evolutionary, singular narrative where the modern constantly supersedes, and therefore makes irrelevant, the traditional and the orthodox,' it would be obliged to see Buddhism as having been superseded by Christianity, Christianity itself by Islam, and Islam by Baha'ism, or Theosophy, or Christian Science. But obviously the FWBO does not see Buddhism as having been superseded by Christianity, merely because Christianity happens to be later. It does not even see Buddhism, in the West, superseding Christianity, and making it irrelevant, merely because it happens to have arrived later on the scene and is new within the Western context. Personally, I do not use the fashionable language of supersession and irrelevance (or relevance) at all, and I doubt if anybody else in the FWBO does. I am a Buddhist, and not a Christian, not because I think that Christianity has now been superseded by the higher path of Buddhism and is no longer relevant. I am a Buddhist because I think that Buddhism is (on the whole) true, and always has been true, and that Christianity is (on the whole) false, and always has been false.

By Christianity I do not mean the liberal Protestantism that, as I have learned from Mellor, rejects doctrines such as the authority of the Church, the Virgin Birth, the Incarnation, and even the existence of God. By Christianity I mean the Christianity of the Creeds and Councils, of the Popes, and of Augustine and Aquinas. In other words, by Christianity I mean traditional, orthodox Christianity, i.e. Roman Catholicism, since it is Roman Catholicism which, as I have already pointed out, has been the normative form of the Christian faith in Western Europe (*vide supra*, p.54). *This* is the Christianity in which I do not believe and which I think false. I do *not* believe in God, the Father almighty, creator of heaven and earth. I do *not* believe in Jesus Christ, his only Son, our Lord. He was *not* conceived of the Virgin Mary, though he may have suffered under Pontius Pilate, may have been crucified, and certainly died and was buried (if he lived at all). He did *not* descend to the dead (*or*, into hell). On the third day he did *not* rise again. He did *not* ascend into heaven, and is *not* seated at the right hand of the Father. He will *not* come again to judge the living and the dead. I do *not* believe in the Holy Spirit, or in the holy catholic Church, or the communion of saints, or the forgiveness of sins (by God through Christ), or the resurrection of the body, or the life everlasting (in heaven). Amen. *Sadhu! Sadhu! Sadhu!*

This is not to say that there is no truth at all in the statements (of the Apostles' Creed) thus negatived. But such truth as they contain is of the symbolic rather than the literal order, especially in the case of such powerfully evocative symbols as the Virgin Birth, the Crucifixion, and the Descent into Hell, some of which have analogues in other religious traditions, including Buddhism. Traditional, orthodox Christianity is certainly aware that its dogmas have a symbolic dimension to them, but this does not prevent it from insisting, at the same time, on the literal and even the historical truth of those dogmas. That they are true means, in effect, that they are literally true.

According to Mellor, dogmatism is among the 'problems' attributed to Christianity by English Buddhists, the charge being one traditionally directed at (Roman) Catholicism by (liberal) Protestants. I have already explained why Western Buddhists, when they criticize Christianity, criticize Roman Catholicism rather than any other form of Western Christianity (*vide supra*, p.54). Since the FWBO sees Christianity not as superseded or irrelevant but as false, there is no question of its being able to 'use both modernist secularization narratives and liberal Protestant Christian complaints about Roman Catholicism [to] support the idea that the world is evolving in a particular direction which leaves traditional Christianity behind,' as Mellor maintains. Nor can it use them to support the view that 'Christianity is now a danger to the individual who wants to develop.' Christianity, as a form of theism, has *always* been a danger to the individual who wants to develop. Any similarity between the FWBO's criticism of Roman Catholicism and liberal Protestant complaints about that form of Christianity are therefore entirely coincidental, and in no way underlines the (supposed) fact 'that western Buddhists and liberal Protestants have a great deal in common'. Starting from the *Brahmajāla-sutta* Buddhism has developed, over the centuries, its own critique of theism and other diṭṭhis or '(speculative) views', and those Western

Buddhists who criticize or attack Roman Catholicism have no need to take their weapons from the arsenal of liberal Protestantism.[33]

3 The FWBO having been convicted of using 'recognizably modernist narratives', Mellor turns to forest monasticism and to the English Sangha. The relation of forest monasticism to modernism is quite different,' he declares. 'The austere asceticism of Ajahn Chah's forest monasteries in Thailand is perhaps, to some degree, a reaction against the phenomenon of "Buddhist modernism".' At this point Mellor hastens to shelter himself beneath the authority of R.J.Z. Werblowsky who, so he assures us, is very critical of Buddhist modernism, and 'highlights its eclecticism, its emphasis on lay participation, and its "glib and naive" assertion that Buddhism is the most "scientific" and the most "modern" of religions.' However, although Werblowsky 'notes' that the origins of such perspectives are in the West (the 'Buddhist modernism' in question is a south-east Asian phenomenon), he does not develop this point in any detail, and Mellor himself goes on to explain that Buddhist modernism is, to some degree, a product of (or response to) Christian influence in Asia, and that it was argued that Buddhism was 'not only more modern than Christianity but more *western*, i.e. rational, scientific and relevant to the modern world.' Confirmation for this explanation is sought from one M. Southwold, who, according to Mellor, has 'noted' how widespread Buddhist modernism is in south-east Asia, and 'its propagation by a westernized middle class.'

Whether it is widespread in south-east Asia or not, I have no sympathy whatever with Buddhist modernism and have never had. Like Werblowsky I am critical of its eclecticism (in the sense of its attempting to combine elements from both Buddhism and science), its emphasis on lay participation, and its assertion that Buddhism is the most scientific and the most modern of religions. Its emphasis on lay participation is, I believe, mistaken, in that it is an emphasis that is given within the framework of the existing monk/lay dichotomy and does nothing to modify that framework. As for its emphasis on the 'scientific' character of Buddhism, I too would describe this as glib and naïve, based as it is on a misunderstanding either of Buddhism or of science or of both. Nevertheless, according to Mellor the relation of forest monasticism to modernism is quite different, i.e. quite different from that of the FWBO. Since he goes on to observe that the austere asceticism of Ajahn Chah's forest monasteries in Thailand 'is, perhaps, to some degree, a reaction against the phenomenon of "Buddhist modernism",' he clearly is connecting the modernism of which he has convicted the FWBO with the Buddhist modernism against which Ajahn Chah's forest monasteries are a reaction and, consequently, connecting the FWBO with that emphasis on the scientific character of Buddhism which, according to Werblowsky, is a feature of Buddhist modernism. Before proceeding to consider the relation of forest monasticism to modernism I must therefore make plain my own and the FWBO's position with regard to the vexed question of the scientific character of Buddhism.

Perhaps I can best do this by adverting to an article I wrote in 1948, when I was still without external guidance and when mistakes in my interpretation of Buddhism might have been expected. This article was entitled 'Buddhism and Science' and was a review of the third edition of P. Lakshmi Narasu's *The Essence of Buddhism*. After commenting on the fact that many people felt a predilection for a work in which the Dharma was expounded in accordance with scientific terminology, I continued:

'This method of exposition does, like every other, furnish certain advantages and entail certain dangers. Of the advantages it would be superfluous to speak, since the undiminished popularity of the book for more than four decades is sufficient testimony on their behalf; but with regard to the dangers a few words may be deemed not out of place.

'The Buddha taught that the Dharma was only a raft to ferry his followers over to the other shore of Nirvana. Japanese Buddhists believe that all teachings are as a finger pointing to the Full Moon of Enlightenment. The Blessed One ironically questioned his disciples whether, after safely reaching the farther bank of a river, they would take the raft on their shoulders and carry it with them out of gratitude to it for having brought them across. Similarly, who will fix his eyes on the pointing finger thinking that it is the Full Moon? Yet the history of religion reveals that men have repeatedly committed exactly this mistake. They have invariably confused the spirit with the letter, have ever fed on the valueless husk rather than the precious kernel, have seen shadow for sunlight, have mistaken the means for the end, the local form for the universal truth, the manner in which a thing is expressed for the mode in which it exists. It is imperative that the truth which is the Buddhadharma should be presented to the men and women of this century not only in the verbal but also in the ideological language with which they are most familiar; but it is of the utmost importance that they should learn to discriminate between the letter which killeth and the spirit which giveth life. The message is not the same as the vehicle by which it is conveyed. The truth of Buddhism as a whole does not coincide with the truth of science. This does not mean that Buddhism contradicts science; it simply affirms that the truth of Buddhism is propounded from the standpoint of that realization which is integral to all experiences whatsoever, whereas the truth of science is advanced from the standpoint of one phase only (the material) of the whole infinite range of experience integrated. Yet, inasmuch as every phase of experience is an integrated factor in the pure, harmonious wholeness of Integral Realization, the integral truth of that realization will be reflected in, and revealed by, the partial truth of the limited experience of every one of the integrated factors. Microcosm mirrors macrocosm. Every jewel in the jewel-net reflects the whole web. If experimental science is able to unearth within its own field of work the puissant presence of those very laws which Buddhism declares to be absolutely universal in scope and operation, then it will have testified to the very limit of its capacity to the truth of the Dharma.'[34]

Thus the youthful Sangharakshita (then known as Anagarika Dharmapriya). Though I would put things differently now, and though I am less sure than I was then of the importance of expounding the Dharma in accordance with scientific terminology, even supposing it to be well understood that (*pace* Marshall McLuhan) the medium is *not* the message, fundamentally my views regarding the 'scientific' character of Buddhism remain unchanged. *The truth of Buddhism as a whole does not coincide with the truth of science.* Broadly speaking there are two levels of existence, that of the composite (*saṁskṛta*) or mundane and that of the incomposite (*asaṁskṛta*) or transcendental, and corresponding to these there are two degrees of knowledge: sense-based rational or scientific knowledge and supra-rational (though not irrational) 'intuitive' knowledge or gnosis   (*prajñā*, i.e. *bhāvanāmayā-prajñā*). While gnosis has access to both levels of existence (to that of the composite, in that it is capable of perceiving its true nature), rational or scientific knowledge has no access to the level of the incomposite or transcendental and is, in fact, completely blind to its existence. Hence there can be no question of equating the (mundane) truth of science with the (transcendental) truth of Buddhism, despite there being a degree of asymmetrical overlap, as we may term it, between them, and no question of identifying scientific knowledge with gnosis on account of similarities between their respective verbal expressions. Much less still can there be any question of proving the truth of Buddhism by appealing to alleged anticipations of modern scientific discoveries, as representatives of Buddhist modernism are wont to do, and neither I nor, so far as I am aware, any member of the FWBO has ever sought to demonstrate the truth of Buddhism in this way or even to recommend Buddhism on such grounds. So much has this been the case that, as I mentioned in connection with the FWBO's alleged suspicion of ritual (*vide supra*, p.66), a leading exponent of Scientific Buddhism actually criticized the FWBO for being 'not related to scientific knowledge'. That the Christian academic should connect the FWBO with Buddhist modernism, while the exponent of Scientific Buddhism should accuse it of being unscientific, is an irony that tells us, perhaps, more about the FWBO's critics than it does about the FWBO.

4 'Ajahn Chah, however, is not interested in being modern: for him, Buddhist truths and traditions are timeless and in no need of being up-dated.' The 'however' is meant to remind us that the relation of forest monasticism to modernism is quite different from the relation of the FWBO to modernism, the latter having been convicted of using 'recognizably modernist narratives' and shown to be connected with south-east Asian Buddhist modernism and its emphasis on the scientific character of Buddhism. Mellor continues: 'Although his [i.e. Ajahn Chah's] movement might also be a response to both external pressures on Buddhism, his approach to the renewal of Buddhism is not based on the desire to make it appear modern, but to *return* to a pristine model of what Buddhism should be. Ajahn Chah is using tradition to purify Buddhism.' This is exactly my own position and the position of the FWBO. One could even adapt Mellor's words, and say, 'Sangharakshita is not interested in being modern: for him, (transcendental) Buddhist truths and (truly Buddhist) traditions are timeless and in no need of being updated (though they may need to be restated in more understandable terms). Although his movement might also be a response to both Christian and pseudo-liberal pressures, his approach to the renewal of Buddhism is not based on the desire to make it appear modern, but to *return* to a pristine model of what Buddhism should be. Sangharakshita is using tradition to purify Buddhism.'

But it is well over a dozen lines since Mellor last appealed for support and confirmation to one of his sociologist mentors, and he now feels the need to do so. 'As Michael Hill has shown, "tradition" often has this radical, creative role, establishing something which is often new, even revolutionary, through the appeal to a golden age, a pristine model, or to the purity of a tradition. Tradition is both a leverage for social change and the signifier of a particular approach to history; that is, history is a narrative of decay interrupted by periods of purification.' I could not agree more. This is exactly how the FWBO sees itself and how it sees (Buddhist) history. Not that the FWBO appeals to a literal 'golden age' of Buddhism, any more than I think Ajahn Chah does (there were disobedient disciples, and disharmony in the Sangha, even in the Buddha's day); but it certainly looks back to, and derives inspiration from, a time when what was of primary importance in the Buddha's teaching was actually treated as primary and what was of secondary importance as secondary. The FWBO's role, like that of tradition in Michael Hill's account, is radical, in the sense of being a return to the spiritual roots of Buddhism, and creative, in the sense of not allowing itself to be determined by the immediate past of British Buddhism or, for the matter of that, by the immediate past of the eastern Buddhist world. Thus the FWBO is engaged in establishing something which, within its immediate context, is new—and, it is hoped, New. It is also a leverage for social change, though this aspect is more apparent in India than in Britain (I shall have something to say about the FWBO's Indian dimension in the following section), and the signifier of a particular approach to history; that is, history as a narrative of decay interrupted by periods of purification, or, as one could equally well say, of purification interrupted by periods of decay.

'It is in this way [i.e. as representing a period of purification] that Ajahn Chah's teacher Ajahn Mun, and Ajahn Chah himself, can be understood as participating in the "revival" of Buddhist meditation practice in the Thai forest monastic tradition.' As Mellor fails to see, it is also the way in which the FWBO can be understood as participating in the revival, in British Buddhist circles, of the practice of Going for Refuge as the central and definitive act of the Buddhist life.

Since the English Sangha has sprung from Ajahn Chah's movement, and Ajahn Chah is not interested in being modern, it follows that the English Sangha has a negative attitude to modernism. Not only that. Since the FWBO 'uses recognizably modernist narratives' it also follows that on the subject of modernism the English Sangha and the FWBO differ. The English Sangha, Mellor assures us, 'is totally opposed to the modernism which is so significant in the FWBO. For the English Sangha, the "modern" is associated with decay rather than progress. Whatever characteristics the English Sangha and the FWBO share, they differ in their attitude to modernism. This has a number of repercussions.' What these repercussions are we shall have to see. They relate mainly to Christianity, to ethics, and to the significance of the individual. Since modernism is *not* significant in the FWBO, however, it may well be that the English Sangha and the FWBO differ less than Mellor supposes and that, where they do differ, it is not on account of the FWBO's (alleged) attitude to modernism.

5 Christianity is treated 'very differently' by the English Sangha and the FWBO. 'Instead of consigning Christianity to a lower stage of evolution,' Mellor informs us with some complacency, 'the English Sangha concentrates on its philosophical differences with Christianity, and often displays quite an appreciative attitude towards it (albeit to a Christianity interpreted firmly within Buddhist categories).' I have already explained that I do not consign Christianity to a lower stage of evolution in the sense of regarding it as having been superseded by Buddhism within an evolutionary, singular narrative where the modern constantly supersedes, and therefore makes irrelevant, the traditional and the orthodox (*vide supra*, p.85 *et seq.*). What the English Sangha's philosophical differences with Christianity are, and where and when it concentrates on them, I am at a loss to understand. Contrary to his usual practice, Mellor gives no references here, and in any case the English Sangha is not known for philosophical activity. Mellor also omits to cite any instance of the appreciative attitude towards Christianity which, according to him, the English Sangha 'often displays'. Not that this really matters. What is really astonishing in the comparison Mellor draws between the English Sangha's treatment of Christianity and that of the FWBO is the parenthesis. The English Sangha often displays an appreciative attitude towards Christianity, *albeit to a Christianity interpreted firmly within Buddhist categories*. Does Mellor realize what he is saying? Does he realize what these categories are, firmly within which Christianity is interpreted by the English Sangha? If the English Sangha is doctrinally orthodox, as I assume it is, then they will be categories deriving, ultimately, from the *Brahmajāla-sutta*, according to which belief in the existence of a Father Almighty, creator of heaven and earth, as asserted in the first clause of the Apostles' Creed, is one of the sixty-two diṭṭhis or '(speculative) views' that must be abandoned if gnosis is to be developed and deliverance from mundane existence achieved. What difference there really is between relegating Christianity to a lower stage of evolution, as the FWBO (allegedly) does, and dismissing Christianity's central tenet as a '(speculative) view', as the English Sangha in effect does, I leave to students of comparative religion to determine.

6 Mellor has rather more to say about differences relating to ethics, the second of the repercussions from the fact that the English Sangha and the FWBO differ in their attitude to modernism. According to him, this is the most important repercussion, the English Sangha being 'markedly separate from the FWBO in its strong emphasis on ethics.' This clearly implies that the FWBO's emphasis on ethics is either weak or non-existent. 'Strong' and 'weak' are, of course, relative terms, and Mellor does not tell us what standard of measurement it is that enables him to ascertain the strength (or weakness) of an ethical emphasis or whether such an emphasis is even present at all. There are two possibilities. Either Mellor is equating ethics with *monastic* ethics or he is equating it with *sexual* ethics. Since the English Sangha is a monastic order, whereas the FWBO (including the WBO) is neither monastic nor lay, it is to be expected that it should emphasize monastic ethics more strongly than does the FWBO; but it would be illogical to infer therefrom that the English Sangha emphasizes ethics *in general* more strongly, and I do not think this is what Mellor is doing. We thus are left with the other possibility: that in asserting that the English Sangha is 'markedly separate from the FWBO in its strong emphasis on ethics' Mellor is equating ethics with sexual ethics. That this is actually the case is borne out by the nature of the evidence he proceeds to produce in support of his thesis. The English Sangha, he assures us, understands contemporary sexual, familial, and social ethics as dangerously lax. 'In contrast, the FWBO encourages the exploration of different types of sexual relationships, sees marriage as a serious handicap to the development of the individual, attacks the "shrill horror and raw vindictiveness" with which certain Christians attack pornography, and always asserts the significance of the individual above the group.' All these are matters of *sexual* ethics, not excluding even the last, with which, as we shall see, Mellor is concerned only to the extent that it impinges on marriage and the family. Nor is that all. In Mellor's enumeration of the FWBO's sexual heresies do we not detect a note of that same shrill horror of which Subhuti speaks? Be that as it may, in connection with his allegation that the FWBO's emphasis on ethics is weak or non-existent there are a number of misunderstandings to be cleared up, as well as one misquotation to be corrected, and I shall therefore (a) refer briefly to my other writings on ethical subjects, (b) comment on the FWBO's sexual heresies as enumerated by Mellor, (c) give a few examples of the FWBO's position on sexual ethics, and (d) indicate the extent of the FWBO's ethical concerns.

(a) Material on (Buddhist) ethics is to be found in all my writings, from *A Survey of Buddhism* (1957) to *A Guide to the Buddhist Path* (1990) and *The Buddha's Victory* (1991). It is even to be found in my writings on art. There are, however, three works which are entirely devoted to the subject. These works are *Aspects of Buddhist Morality, Vision and Transformation,* and *The Ten Pillars of Buddhism.* In *Aspects of Buddhist Morality* (1978) I discuss the nature of morality, morality and the spiritual ideal, morality mundane and transcendental, patterns of morality, the benefits of morality, and determinants of morality. *Vision and Transformation* (1990, but based on lectures given in 1969) is devoted to the Buddha's Noble Eightfold Path, with Vision representing the first step or stage (*aṅga*, literally 'limb') and Transformation the seven remaining steps or stages. *The Ten Pillars of Buddhism* (1984), a disquisition on the Ten Precepts, is divided into two parts. In Part I I deal with the Ten Precepts collectively, under such headings as the Relation between the Refuges and Precepts, the Ten Precepts as Principles of Ethics, and the Ten Precepts as Rules of Training; in Part II I deal with them individually. Since ordination into the Western Buddhist Order consists in Going for Refuge to the Buddha, Dharma, and Sangha, *and* in undertaking to observe the Ten Precepts (as well as having the effectiveness of one's Going for Refuge 'witnessed' by experienced senior members of the Order), the Ten Precepts obviously occupy a position of central importance in the life of the FWBO, as indeed they (or the Five or the Eight Precepts) do in the life of all genuinely Buddhist groups. It is therefore not surprising that I should speak of them as the Ten

Pillars of Buddhism, or that I should eulogize them in the following terms:

> 'The Ten Precepts are, indeed, the massy supports of the entire majestic edifice of the Dharma. Without the Ten Precepts the Dharma could not, in fact, exist. Continuing the architectural metaphor, one might say that the Three Jewels are the three-stepped plinth and foundation of the Dharma, the Ten Precepts the double row of pillars supporting the spacious dome, Meditation the dome itself, and Wisdom the lofty spire that surmounts the dome. Elaborating, one might say that each of the ten pillars was made of a precious stone or precious metal, so that there was a pillar of diamond, a pillar of gold, a pillar of crystal, and so on. In this way we should be able to gain not only an understanding of the importance of the Ten Precepts but also, perhaps, an appreciation of their splendour and beauty.'[35]

It is also not surprising that *The Ten Pillars of Buddhism* should be a prescribed text for postulants of the Western Buddhist Order (*Vision and Transformation* is included in the three-year Mitra Study Course). What *is* surprising is that Mellor, ignoring this work and my other writings on ethical subjects, should see the FWBO as not emphasizing ethics. If giving the Ten Precepts a position of central importance in one's life, and eulogizing them as necessary to the Dharma's very existence, does not constitute an emphasis on ethics it is difficult to know what would.

(b) 'The FWBO encourages the exploration of different types of sexual relationships.' Here Mellor refers to *Buddhism for Today*, p.167. On looking up the reference, however, we find that Subhuti is not speaking of sexual relationships, and that it is not the exploration of different types of *sexual* relationships that the FWBO encourages. What Subhuti actually says is: 'It should be possible for everyone to have a wide range of relationships of different kinds in which all his needs, biological, psychological, social, and spiritual can be met without conflict'—a very different thing. Mellor has not only attributed to Subhuti views he does not hold; he has also misinterpreted the FWBO. No doubt the reason for his so doing is that he equates ethics with sexual ethics and assumes, therefore, that 'relationships' means *sexual* relationships. Subhuti continues: 'Each person should be part of a network within which all these various needs can be met without overloading any one particular relationship.' We shall come back to this point when I give examples of the FWBO's position on sexual ethics.

'[The FWBO] sees marriage as a serious handicap to the development of the individual.' Here Mellor again refers us to *Buddhism for Today*, p.166, but though he does not actually misquote Subhuti (apart from substituting his own 'serious handicap' for Subhuti's 'barrier') he is far from doing justice to the latter's temperate and balanced three-page discussion of the relation between the individual and the family. In any case, it is surprising that for Mellor seeing marriage as a serious handicap to the development of the individual (i.e. the individual-in-relation-to-Buddhahood) should be one of the repercussions of *modernism*. As Subhuti reminds us, 'the young Buddha-to-be left behind his social position, his wealth, his parents, even his wife and son,' and as it should not be necessary for me to remind Mellor, Jesus never married and seems not to have considered the family to be an important or significant institution. Moreover, Mellor is contrasting the English Sangha's 'strong emphasis on ethics', i.e. sexual ethics, with the FWBO's weak or non-existent emphasis. But the English Sangha is a monastic order. Its members have renounced sex, marriage, and family life, at least for the time being (in Buddhism monastic vows are not taken for life). How is it, then, that Mellor sees the English Sangha and the FWBO as differing in their attitude to modernism, at least as regards (sexual) ethics? It is possible, of course, that the contradiction is not so much in Mellor himself as in the English Sangha, which although a celibate body seems to give

guarded approval to legal marriage and the nuclear family—
perhaps because it sees them as the only alternative to sexual
anarchy. There is also the fact that a monastic order is economically dependent on the laity and cannot afford to depreciate the
latter's chosen way of life beyond a certain point; but this is a
consideration pertaining to an area of ethics with which we are
not now concerned.

'[The FWBO] attacks the "shrill horror and raw vindictiveness"
with which certain Christians attack pornography.' Once again
we are referred to *Buddhism for Today*, this time to p.77. Mellor
also adds a note. 'Although Subhuti does not explicitly state that
the FWBO approves of pornography, this passage [from *Buddhism for Today*] seems to imply that any limitations on an
individual's right to experience different forms of sex-related activities (including the consumption or production of pornography) are to be opposed.' The passage implies no such thing.
It implies no such thing because the FWBO does not discuss ethical questions in terms of rights. As long ago as 1951 I expressed
the view that rights and duties are inseparable and that if all
men did their duty to one another it would not be necessary
even to speak of rights. Duties rather than rights were therefore
to be emphasized.[36] Since then I have developed this line of
thought further. I believe that 'rights' is not an ethical concept
(though 'duties' is), but only a legal one. Ethically speaking, the
individual has no rights. Hence there can be no question, from
the FWBO's point of view, of an individual's *right* to experience
different forms of sex-related activities (including the consumption or production of pornography) and no question, therefore,
of Subhuti implying that any limitations on such a right are to
be opposed. From the FWBO's point of view the real question is
whether the consumption or production of pornography is conducive to the observance of the third precept, the precept of
abstention from sexual misconduct (and cultivation of content-
ment). Order members and Mitras are, I think, generally agreed
that it is not conducive. Whether the consumption or production

of pornography should be illegal is a different matter altogether. It has not been discussed within the Order, so far as I know, and I personally do not hold definite views on either side of the question.

Mellor is therefore wrong in concluding, as he does in the last sentence of his note, that 'the FWBO approaches sex-related issues through liberationist discourse and favours leaving moral decisions to individuals.' The FWBO favours leaving moral decisions to individuals because it is only to individuals that, in the last resort, moral decisions *can* be left (even the decision to follow tradition, or the teaching of the Church, is a moral decision inasmuch as it is a decision to do what one believes is *right*). In practice this means, within the FWBO itself, that moral decisions are left to the individual-in-relation-to-Buddhahood, and that he makes his decision in the light of his commitment to the Three Jewels and in consultation with spiritual friends, both horizontal and vertical. As for Mellor's charge that the FWBO approaches sex-related issues through liberationist discourse, let me conclude my observations on his note with an extract from the 1951 essay (on 'Rights and Duties') to which I have already referred and which I probably wrote before Mellor was born and long before he immersed himself in the confusions of theory and methodology.

'The word for duty and the word for religion (which consists at bottom in the eradication of the ego-sense) are, in the languages of India, one word: Dharma. But the clamourous insistence upon our rights, upon what is legally, morally, or even spiritually due from others to us, only strengthens greed, strengthens desire, strengthens selfishness, strengthens egotism.

'The performance of one's duties results in the establishment of love and peace, the attempted extortion of one's rights in the outbreak of hatred and violence. Duties unite, rights divide. Duties are co-operative, rights competitive.

The former depend upon our own selves, and are therefore swift and easy of accomplishment; the latter depend on others, and are therefore tardy and difficult, if not impossible, of achievement. Rights are wrested forcibly from other human beings outside, but duties are softly and sweetly laid upon us by the voice of the Divine—of our own potential Buddhahood—reverberating within.

'Buddhism, being based upon the realization of emptiness, upon egolessness, upon unselfishness, teaches the doctrine of the mutual interpenetration of all things, inculcates the practice of love and compassion, exhorts men and women to perform their duties in every walk of life, and therefore tends naturally towards the ultimate establishment of peace, both in the hearts and minds of men and in the world of events outside us. Western political systems, on the contrary, however different or even antagonistic they may outwardly seem, are all based upon the concept, ultimately of dogmatic Christian origin, of the existence of separate, mutually exclusive ego-entities which are socially, politically, and even spiritually valuable and significant in themselves. All such systems therefore justify hatred and excuse violence, all insist on the intrinsic reasonableness of clamourous agitation for rights, and all therefore, without exception—despite emphatic protestations to the contrary—result in the eventual outbreak of war, both in the individual psyche and in the life of societies and nations.'[37]

If these words were true forty years ago, they are even truer today.

However, we must not forget that Mellor is citing the fact that the FWBO 'attacks the "shrill horror and raw vindictiveness" with which certain Christians attack pornography' as evidence in support of his thesis that, in contrast to the 'strong emphasis' of the English Sangha, the FWBO's emphasis on (sexual) ethics is weak or non-existent. But Subhuti is concerned with sexual ethics only indirectly. What he is doing is attacking the pseudo-ethical moralism of traditional, orthodox Christianity—a moralism by which, he believes, sexual morality has been made impossibly complex for most Westerners. This is not evidence of a weak or non-existent emphasis on (sexual) ethics. If it is evidence of anything, it is evidence of a different kind of ethical emphasis, in the light of which the 'shrill horror and raw vindictiveness' with which certain Christians attack pornography is seen as being no more ethical than the pornography they attack.

Finally, '[the FWBO] always asserts the significance of the individual above the group.' Mellor apparently regards this as evidence of the weakness or non-existence of the FWBO's emphasis on (sexual) ethics because, as he goes on to explain, 'the FWBO seeks the destruction of traditional sexual and social structures, while the English Sangha would like to see them strengthened.' This enables him to conclude, 'The FWBO is modernist, while for the English Sangha what is modern is generally associated with decadence.' Leaving aside the question of whether the English Sangha would really like to see a strengthening of the banks, the public schools, and the trade unions, for example, as well as of legal marriage and the nuclear family, let us see in what manner the FWBO 'asserts the significance of the individual above the group'. But this is a question which chimes with the third of the repercussions from the fact that (according to Mellor) the English Sangha and the FWBO differ in their attitude to modernism, and I propose to deal with it when we come to that repercussion. Before proceeding to give a few examples of the FWBO's position on sexual ethics, however, I would like to make a comment on Mellor's statement, 'The FWBO is modernist, while for the English Sangha what is modern is generally associated with decadence.'

Writers on modernism generally distinguish between modernism and modernity. The fact that (according to Mellor) the English Sangha and the FWBO differ in their attitude to modernism does not necessarily mean that they differ in their attitude to modernity or that the English Sangha does, in fact, associate the modern (as distinct from modernism) with decadence. Indeed it would be strange if it did so, for though it belongs to the Thai forest tradition its members very sensibly live in houses, operate personal bank accounts, make use of gas and electricity, and rely on modern transport.

(c) My examples of the FWBO's position on sexual ethics relate to (i) the sexual relationship, (ii) abortion, (iii) homosexuality, and (iv) celibacy or chastity.

(i) The FWBO does not see the sexual relationship as being the principal relationship in human life. On the contrary, it believes that the true individual, or individual-in-relation-to-Buddhahood, will relegate his sexual relationships to a position nearer the periphery than the centre of his personal mandala (to use the FWBO idiom), the centre of the mandala being occupied, so far as human relationships are concerned, by spiritual friendships, both horizontal and vertical. This means that the FWBO does not subscribe to that idealization, romanticization, and, as we may say, pseudo-spiritualization, of the sexual relationship which is so marked a feature of modern Western culture and which has even invaded the realm of serious religious thought. To take an example at random: commenting on Karl Barth's assertion that sexuality is 'the basic form of all association and fellowship, which is the essence of humanity', the philosopher and theologian John Macquarrie observes '[sexuality is so interpreted] because the sexual relation is the most intimate act of mutual self-giving and communion possible for two human beings. Indeed, can we still speak of "two"? Or have they become in a sense a new whole—"one flesh" in the biblical language?'[38]

It is partly because of its belief that the true individual relegates his sexual relationships to a position nearer the periphery of his personal mandala that the FWBO encourages the exploration of different types of relationships. These are not *sexual* relationships, as Mellor wrongly asserts, but a range of relationships of *different kinds* in which, in the words of Subhuti, everyone's needs, biological, psychological, social, and spiritual can be met without conflict (*vide supra*, p.98). The scriptural basis for the FWBO's view that, as Subhuti goes on to say, each person should be part of a network within which all these various needs can be met without overloading any one particular relationship, is the *Sigalovada-sutta*. In this sutta, which is widely studied in the FWBO, the Buddha teaches the young brahmin Sigala the *right* way to worship the six quarters of earth and sky. He should revere his mother and father as the eastern quarter, his teacher as the southern quarter, his wife as the western quarter, his friends and counsellors as the northern quarter, his slaves and servants as the lower quarter, and ascetics and brahmans as the upper quarter, and he should revere each of them in five ways, all of which are explained in detail.[39] Here we truly have a network within which the individual's biological, psychological, social, and spiritual needs can be met without overloading any particular relationship.

In the modern West, however, we have no such network. As the quotation from John Macquarrie suggests, our reverence is directed too exclusively to the western quarter. We overload the sexual relationship, in the sense of making greater emotional demands on it than it is capable of meeting, with the result that other relationships are neglected and the sexual relation itself is put under severe strain. Besides encouraging the exploration of different types of relationships generally, the FWBO therefore recommends the cultivation of two other relationships in particular, partly for their own sakes and partly in order to take some of the strain off the sexual relationship. It encourages the individual to direct his reverence not only to the western quarter but also to the eastern and northern quarters. It encourages him to cultivate his relationship with his mother and father and his relationship with his friends and counsellors. (Reverence for the northern quarter, of cultivation of one's relationship with ascetics and brahmans, is encouraged only so far as it represents the cultivation of vertical spiritual friendship.)

The individual's relationship with his (or her) friends and counsellors in fact receives a good deal of attention in the FWBO. Texts on friendship from various traditions are studied, and there is a series of nine lectures on 'Spiritual Friendship' by Subhuti which cover virtually all aspects of the subject. The individual's relationship to his (or her) parents receives rather less attention, though it is by no means neglected. As I have noticed since coming back to Britain, in the West children are often on bad terms with one parent or the other, or with both, sometimes even feeling anger and resentment towards them. The FWBO therefore emphasizes the importance of being on good terms with one's parents, for everybody's sake, and encourages its members to transform any negative feelings they may have towards their parents into positive ones. Some Order members and Mitras report a marked improvement in their relationship with their parents since they became involved with the FWBO, and I suspect that the relationship which FWBO members enjoy with their parents is on the whole more harmonious than that enjoyed by any comparable group of people in the wider community.

(ii) Abortion or the deliberate termination of pregnancy before the foetus is viable constitutes an infraction of the first precept, that of abstention from taking life, and there can be no question of a female Order member (for example) undergoing an abortion or a male or female Order member or Mitra performing an abortion, or encouraging one, or even approving one. Women who have had an abortion prior to becoming involved with the FWBO will be asked to recognize that they have acted unskilfully, to confess their unskilfulness to their spiritual friends, and to resolve not to commit an unskilful action of this kind again. The FWBO does not agree that abortion is a woman's right. As already explained, I do not believe that 'rights' is an ethical concept, and in any case there cannot be an *ethical* right to perform an unethical action, though there may be a legal one.

(iii) Traditional, orthodox Christianity has a horror of homosexuality, the vice 'not to be named among Christians', and besides inflicting untold suffering on homosexuals has bequeathed a legacy of neurotic homophobia to practically the entire Western world. The FWBO demonstrates no continuities with these perspectives, as Mellor would say. It does not discriminate against people on account of their sexual orientation, any more than it discriminates against them on account of their age, their class, their race, or their national origin. On the contrary, it welcomes all, would befriend all, and seeks to introduce all to the riches of the Dharma. It does this, in the case of homosexual men and women, as a matter of common justice to a beleaguered minority, and because conscious or unconscious fear of homosexuality is one of the factors preventing (heterosexual) men, in particular, from forming deep and emotionally satisfying friendships with members of their own sex. As Stuart Miller notes, 'The fear of homosexuality and how it affects the possibilities of male friendship in our times are topics that need contemplating.... The estate of male friendship—indeed, of nearly all human relationships—is sufficiently sunk that mere sex remains at the centre of people's imaginations. The only moving human relationships that people seem able to conjure up are the erotic ones.'[40] And again, 'Deep friendship between adult men is quite rare in our society.'[41] Thus the FWBO's position on homosexuality relates as much to the development of (non-sexual) male friendship as it does to homosexuality itself, and it relates to the development of male friendship because of the vital importance of spiritual friendship in the Buddhist life.

(iv) The FWBO not only believes that the true individual will relegate his sexual relationships to the periphery of his personal mandala; it also believes that, regardless of sexual orientation, he will move in the direction of celibacy or chastity. Celibacy is the state or condition of being unmarried; chastity is abstention from sexual intercourse. Both words translate the Indo-Aryan term brahmacharya, which has connotations of celibate student-hood and religious chastity. Literally, the term means 'faring in the Divine' and is the archaic Buddhist expression for what nowadays we would call the spiritual life. Since members of the Western Buddhist Order are neither monks or nuns nor lay people the Order does not divide into those who practise, or try to practise, celibacy/chastity, and those who do not. All Order members move in the direction of brahmacharya, however slowly they do so and however distant the goal may be. Brahmacharya is not an absolute, particularly when it is seen as being verbal and mental as well as physical: it is a matter of degree, so that there is no question of passing from a state of complete non-brahmacharya to a state of complete brahmacharya at a single bound. Moving in the direction of brahmacharya means practising, or trying to practise, brahmacharya to a greater and ever greater degree. Moreover, the practice of brahmacharya is not only a matter of abstinence from sexual activity; it also involves the enjoyment of higher, progressively more 'divine' levels of consciousness wherein, as I explain in *The Ten Pillars of Buddhism*, one transcends the state of sexual dimorphism and lives an 'angelic' life of spiritual androgynousness.[42]

(d) The extent of the FWBO's ethical concerns is indicated by the fact that Order members undertake to observe the Ten Precepts and that these 'Ten Pillars of Buddhism', as I call them, are the subject of intensive study within the Movement. It is also indicated by the fact that Order members and Mitras alike are encouraged to follow the Noble Eightfold Path, and thus gradually to transform each and every aspect of their lives in the light of Right Understanding or Perfect Vision (*samyag-dṛṣṭi*). Both these traditional formulations, that of the Ten Precepts and that of the Noble Eightfold Path, are quite comprehensive in scope, particularly the latter, the more especially since both cover social as well as personal ethics. They certainly do not equate ethics with sexual ethics, in the way Mellor does (*vide supra*, p.96. Though sexual ethics are by no means neglected, these constitute only a small part of each formulation, being the subject matter of the Third Precept, that of abstention from sexual misconduct (*kamesu-micchācāra*), and a portion of the first step or stage (*aṅga*, literally 'limb') of the Noble Eightfold Path, that of Right or Perfect Action (*samyak-karmānta*).

While in principle Order members observe abstention from killing, abstention from taking the not-given, and the rest of the Ten Precepts, equally, and while Order members and Mitras are encouraged to traverse all eight steps or stages of the Noble Eightfold Path, in practice certain precepts or certain steps or stages are emphasized more than others, at least in the sense of their being the objects of a greater amount of attention and discussion. One such emphasis is on the First Precept, that of abstention from killing, as represented by the practice of excluding meat and fish from one's diet. The vast majority of Order members are vegetarians, and a few are vegans, and they find it difficult to understand why so many Eastern Buddhists (including monks belonging to the Thai forest tradition), should be unable, apparently, to see any connection between eating meat and fish and the killing of living beings. In Britain, however, an increasingly large number of people do see a connection between them, and one of the ways in which the FWBO encourages vegetarianism, and thus the observance of the First Precept, is by running vegetarian restaurants. This does not mean that the FWBO regards vegetarianism and spiritual life as being virtually synonymous, as do certain orthodox Hindus. Much less still does it mean that the FWBO believes that absolute abstention from the killing of living beings (including microbes) is a real possibility, even for vegetarians and vegans. Health and economics apart, the FWBO encourages vegetarianism for two reasons. It encourages it in order to reduce the amount of animal suffering, and it encourages it as a means of affirming the principle of non-violence in today's increasingly violent society. Were the FWBO to equate ethics with non-violence in the way

Mellor equates it with sexual ethics, one could reverse his pronouncement regarding the differences between the English Sangha and the FWBO relating to ethics (*vide supra*, p.96), and say, 'The FWBO is markedly separate from the (non-vegetarian) English Sangha in its strong emphasis on ethics.'

Though the FWBO runs vegetarian restaurants, and runs them as a means of encouraging observance of the First Precept, as represented by vegetarianism, it does not run them on the usual commercial lines. It runs them as what it terms team-based Right Livelihood businesses. As such they form part of the FWBO's emphasis on Right or Perfect Livelihood (*samyak-ājiva*), the fourth step or stage of the Noble Eightfold Path. Thus the FWBO's vegetarian restaurants embody a double ethical emphasis, on the First Precept, that of abstention from killing, and also on Right or Perfect Livelihood. Traditionally, Right or Perfect Livelihood means gaining one's living by fair methods, without resorting to deceit, treachery, soothsaying, trickery, or usury. More specifically, it means not engaging in the five trades prohibited to all Buddhists: trading in arms, in living beings, in flesh, in intoxicating liquors, and in poison—military service, and the work of hunter, fisherman, etc. being understood as also included in the list.

During the last ten or twelve years the FWBO has developed this basic concept in a number of ways, some of them with implications for other aspects of the ethical and spiritual life, with the result that Right or Perfect Livelihood is now represented, for the FWBO, by its team-based Right Livelihood businesses. A team-based Right Livelihood business provides the Order member or Mitra who works in it with three things. (a) The means of meeting his material needs, including those of any dependants. (b) Work that does no harm, either physical or mental, to himself or to others, and which leaves him time for rest, meditation, and social and cultural activities. (c) An environment conducive to his development as a (true) individual, especially one that provides him with opportunities for living and working with other people and developing spiritual friendships. No less importantly, a team-based Right Livelihood business also applies its profits to the support of FWBO activities.

Besides vegetarian restaurants, the FWBO runs wholefood stores, gift shops, a publishing house, an export-import business, and a gardening service—all on the same team-based Right Livelihood principles. That it runs so many businesses, of such widely different kinds, means that the FWBO is obliged to concern itself with all sorts of questions of business ethics. These questions are often the subject of intense discussion within the businesses immediately concerned, and if they are of sufficient general interest they may also be discussed within the wider Movement. Some of the questions with which the FWBO has to concern itself are questions of relevance to businesses in the outside world, and Order members with business backgrounds have begun investigating the whole subject of business ethics within this broader context. Following the recent crop of disclosures of unethical dealings on a grand scale in the upper echelons of business and finance, some British businessmen have become more alive to the importance of business ethics, and it may well be that the FWBO, with its emphasis on Right or Perfect Livelihood, particularly as represented by its team-based Right Livelihood businesses, is in a position to contribute to the debate. Were the FWBO to equate ethics with business ethics in the way Mellor equates it with sexual ethics, one could again reverse his pronouncement regarding the differences between the English Sangha and the FWBO relating to ethics (*vide supra*, p.96), this time saying, 'The FWBO is markedly separate from the (economically inactive) English Sangha in its strong ethical emphasis.'

The FWBO also emphasizes Right or Perfect Awareness (*samyak-smṛti*), the seventh step or stage of the Noble Eightfold Path, as represented by awareness of the natural environment, though it emphasizes it less strongly than vegetarianism or team-based Right Livelihood or, indeed, some of the other levels of awareness. Our attitude towards natural objects should be untainted by subjectivity. As I say elsewhere, 'We should learn to look, learn to see, learn to be aware, and in this way become supremely receptive.'[43] An aware attitude will also be a responsible one. That is, it will be an ethical attitude and, as such, one involving a serious grappling with environmental issues.

7 Having contrasted the FWBO's weak or non-existent emphasis on ethics with the English Sangha's 'strong emphasis', Mellor goes on to point out that there is 'a marked divergence in the significance of the individual in each set of discourses.' This is the third repercussion from the fact that the English Sangha and the FWBO differ in their attitude to modernism, and echoes what Mellor has already said about the FWBO always asserting the significance of the individual above that of the group (*vide supra*, p.103). 'For the FWBO the evolution of the individual is the "point" of history, so that all that is perceived to inhibit individual development is regarded with hostility.' But who is this individual whose evolution is the 'point' of history and whose significance is above that of the group? He is not what I call the group member, or statistical individual, as Mellor seems to think. Rather is he the true individual, or the individual-in-relation-to-Buddhahood, and it is true individuals who constitute the spiritual community, just as it is statistical individuals who make up the group. Thus we have four categories: the group member or statistical individual, the group, the true individual, and the spiritual community. To these I sometimes add a fifth category, that of the positive group, which is not so much a separate and distinct kind of group as that aspect of the group which helps rather than hinders individual development, at least to the extent of not actively opposing it. Were the FWBO actually to speak of the evolution of the individual as being the 'point' of history (and neither I nor Subhuti speak of it in this way), it would be only in the sense that the true individual arises in dependence on the group member, just as the higher evolution arises in dependence on the lower evolution and the first stage of the transcendental Path on the last stage of the mundane path.

Mellor seems unable to imagine a state of affairs in which group and (true) individual are in conflict. This is because he has only two categories, that of the group (as I term it)/society/tradition/Church and that of the individualist who, quite wrongly as he evidently thinks, rejects the authority of the group/society/tradition/Church and refuses to be bound by it. In other words, Mellor's categories are reductively sociological (quite early on in his article he uses language that suggests he views 'religions' as having only a social and cultural existence [*vide supra*, p.19]), and it is because his categories are reductively sociological and exclude the category of the true individual that he is unable to imagine Christianity and the nuclear family as inhibiting individual development, i.e. the development of the true individual, and unable to imagine them as being rightly attacked for so doing. When Subhuti criticizes Christianity and the nuclear family, therefore, as he does in *Buddhism for Today* (though not so one-sidedly as Mellor's rather selective quotations suggest), Mellor can see in this only a manifestation of anti-social, even antinomian, individualism. 'Hence, in spite of the Buddhist concept of non-self,' he concludes, after his final quotation from *Buddhism for Today*, 'the FWBO appears an exceptionally individualistic movement.'

The English Sangha presents a much brighter picture, even though one less bright than Mellor could have wished. But before we move on to this picture I must correct what seems to be an erroneous assumption on Mellor's part. Having noted that the nuclear family is an object of hostility to the FWBO 'because it is understood to put limits on individual development,' and having given instances of Subhuti's criticism of it on this score, he proceeds to quote Subhuti on the subject of the divorce rate. '"The mounting divorce rate",' Subhuti is represented as saying, 'is "to be rejoiced in as a sign of wholesale disaffection" from the unhealthy intensity of marriage and the nuclear family.' Leaving aside the circumstance that what Subhuti actually says is that the mounting divorce rate is to be rejoiced in 'from a certain point of view', the fact that Mellor should see such rejoicing as a manifestation of individualism, and therefore as being opposed to group/society/tradition/Church, shows he assumes that what is traditional in (Roman Catholic) Christianity is likewise traditional in Buddhism and that, conversely, what is untraditional in the one is also untraditional in the other. But this is by no means the case. Divorce is *not* untraditional in Buddhism, and the fact that Subhuti can rejoice in the mounting divorce rate is no more a signaller that the FWBO is individualistic than would be his rejoicing in an increase in polygyny and polyandry, neither of which is untraditional in Buddhism.

The greater brightness of the picture presented by the English Sangha is owing to the fact that, according to Mellor, 'the concept of non-self occupies a prominent position in [its] discourse.' History is not an upward spiral but a downward one, he explains on the English Sangha's behalf, and therefore the individualism of Western society needs eliminating not developing. The FWBO would certainly agree that the individualism of Western society needs eliminating. All its activities, from the cultivation of spiritual friendship to the practice of the recollection of the Six Elements, are directed to this end. But it would not agree that history is a downward spiral (has humanity been only spiralling downwards since history began?). History consists of both upward and downward spirals, either one of which may predominate at any given time without ever gaining a permanent ascendancy, though the higher reaches of an upward spiral may at times support, in the person of the true individual, a supra-historical transcendental 'continuation'. However, the concept of history as a constant downward spiral would seem to represent Mellor's own reading of the English Sangha's position (he gives no reference here), and I would prefer to stay with the fact that for the English

Sangha individualism is something to be eliminated, especially as Mellor goes on to observe that 'Ajahn Sumedho sees society as "a group of individual human beings" rather than as a genuinely collective, transpersonal reality.' It is as a group of individual human beings that the FWBO, too, sees society, though it also sees it as consisting of group members, or statistical individuals, who are in the majority, and true individuals, who are in the minority. The concept of society as a genuinely collective, transpersonal reality has been dealt with already. As I pointed out in connection with the individual's efforts to create conditions more favourable to the eradication of mental defilements, efforts which may involve the repudiation of 'transpersonal social forms (such as the Church)', it is necessary to distinguish between what is horizontally transpersonal and what is vertically transpersonal (*vide supra*, p.37).

It is Ajahn Sumedho's failure to see society as being anything other than 'a group of individual human beings', so that for him (as for the FWBO) 'there is no "social world" in Richard Sennett's sense of the term', that detracts from the brightness of the picture presented by the English Sangha as compared with the individualistic FWBO. In respect of its concept of society, Mellor regretfully concludes, the English Sangha is in step with the general cultural orientation towards the individual in the contemporary West. However, he is able to console himself with the reflection that within this orientation 'Ajahn Sumedho demonstrates a very different approach to issues like the significance of the individual in relation to the family.' The nature of this approach is illustrated by a passage from one of Ajahn Sumedho's public talks, on 'The Family'. 'Rather than the family, we tend to think of ourselves,' declares the Ajahn, presumably in ringing tones.... 'We've been given free-rein to develop our lives as much as we want to. Whether my family, my parents, like it or not doesn't matter. Whether it's disgracing the family name has never occurred to me. My background, my conditioning, has been one of "develop yourself", be a self-sufficient, independent person ... a *personality*.' A damning indictment in-deed, and one can almost see the curl of Ajahn Sumedho's lip, and the condemnatory gleam in his eye, as he emphasizes the shocking word 'personality'. It is an indictment very much to Mellor's liking. It enables him to comment that, in this passage, 'western society is not a series of dangerous oppressions, but dangerous liberations,' and that, 'The apparent obsession with the individual makes contemporary life "a neurotic and mean-ingless existence".' It also enables him to conclude, no doubt to his own satisfaction, that the difference between the English Sangha and the FWBO in respect of the significance of the in-dividual in relation to the family is rooted in competing under-standings of history. 'The English Sangha sees itself as working against the grain of western culture, rather than as the pinnacle of a long evolutionary development.' Once again there are a number of misunderstandings to be cleared up. I shall consider them in relation to (a) the individual and the family, (b) the in-dividual and liberation, and (c) the individual and evolution.

(a) When Ajahn Sumedho declares, 'Rather than the family, we tend to think of ourselves,' it is presumably the individualist to whom he is referring. It is the individualist whom he sees as having been given freedom to develop, regardless of his family's wishes and regardless of whether it disgraces the family name. It is the individualist whose background and conditioning has been one of 'develop yourself, be a self-sufficient, independent person ... a *personality*.' As a critique of individualism this is un-exceptionable, and the FWBO would endorse every word of it, though perhaps without giving the same pejorative emphasis to the word 'personality'. But what of the true individual, or in-dividual-in-relation-to-Buddhahood? He, too, has been given the freedom to develop his life, and he, too, may choose to develop it in such a way as to bring disgrace, real or imagined, on the family name, even though in his case he will be aware of what he is doing. Ajahn Sumedho appears to believe that one who comes into conflict with his family cannot but be an individualist, and he appears to believe this because he fails to distinguish the individualist from the true individual, just as Mellor fails to do. It is almost as if he was arguing that since the individualist comes into conflict with his family one who comes into conflict with his family must be an individualist. But I do not want to make too much of this. Mellor may be quoting Ajahn Sumedho out of context, and the latter in any case is presumably speaking without reference to the FWBO. I shall therefore take the passage at its face value, so to speak, as though it had not been extracted from a talk by Ajahn Sumedho and as though Mellor had not produced it as evidence of the way in which the English Sangha's approach to the family differs from that of the individualistic FWBO.

Let me take for my starting point the notion of disgracing the family name. To disgrace means to bring shame and discredit upon, but whether the way in which one chooses to develop one's life disgraces the family name will depend upon the nature of the family and what it is that they consider to be shameful and discreditable. A philistine family will feel disgraced if one of its members becomes an artist, while a criminal family will feel disgraced if one of its members becomes a policeman. It could, of course, be argued that the artist and the policeman are being individualistic, and should *not* have disgraced their families in the way they did, but this would be straining logic. A family has not necessarily been disgraced, at least not in real ethical terms, because it feels shamed and discredited by the behaviour of one of its members. Indeed, it may feel disgraced when it is in fact being highly honoured. The paradigmatic examples of individuals who have 'disgraced' their families in this way are the Buddha and Jesus. The Buddha disgraced his noble and wealthy family by begging in the streets of Kapilavastu, and was reproached by his father for so doing. Jesus disgraced *his* family by preaching and healing, with the result that 'his relatives heard of this and set out to take charge of him, convinced that he was out of his mind.' (Thus *The Jerusalem Bible*.[44] *The*

Unvarnished Gospels has, '"He's gone mad!"[45])'. Unless one is prepared to argue that the Buddha and Jesus were individualists (as some modern defenders of the family no doubt would) one has to recognize that living in a way that disgraces the family name does not necessarily mean that 'Rather than the family, we tend to think of ourselves,' and therefore does not necessarily mean that we are individualists. The reason that the Buddha 'disgraced' his family by begging in the streets was that begging in this way was, as he explained to his irate father, the custom of his race, the race in question being not the mortal Shakyan lineage into which he had been born but the deathless Buddha-lineage into which he had been adopted by virtue of his own attainment of Supreme Enlightenment.[46] The customs of the group are superseded by the customs of the spiritual family, just as the group itself is superseded by the spiritual family or spiritual community.

But what does 'thinking of ourselves' mean? If living in a way that disgraces the family name does not necessarily mean that we are individualists, then, presumably, thinking of ourselves rather than of the family does not necessarily mean that we are individualists either. The truth is that the phrase is ambiguous. It is ambiguous because 'ourselves' is ambiguous. Is this self of ours of which we tend to think, rather than thinking of the family, the group-member self, or is it the true-individual self? If it is the group-member self, then 'thinking of myself' rather than of the family will represent a conflict between one part of the group and another, with the family thinking of itself, rather than of me, in much the same way that I think of myself rather than of the family. Here the conflict is horizontal. If on the other hand the self of which I tend to think is the true-individual self, then 'thinking of myself' rather than of the family will represent a conflict between the true individual and the group, with the family thinking of itself, rather than of me, but thinking of itself in a way very different from the way in which I think of myself. Here the conflict is vertical. If the self of which I am thinking when I think of myself rather than of the family is the true-individual self, I will use the free-rein I've been given to develop my life 'as much as I want to' in a way that is not subjective and self-indulgent (i.e. indulgent of the group-member self or statistical individual) but which will help me to progress towards Enlightenment (*bodhi*). Whether my family, my parents, like it or not will certainly not be a matter of indifference to me. If they do not like the way in which I am using my free-rein I will explain why I believe it is the best way for me to live. In any case, I will keep in touch with them and assist them in any way I can. Should they feel I am disgracing the family name I will explain in what real disgrace consists. If my background, my conditioning, has been one of 'develop yourself, be a self-sufficient, independent person ... a *personality*' in an individualistic sense, I will create a new background, a new, spiritually-positive conditioning, and do my best to be a true individual, an individual-in-relation-to-Buddhahood. I will be self-sufficient in the sense of taking from others as little as I can, and giving as much as I can, and independent in the sense of not allowing others to do for me what I can do for myself and doing for them what they are unable to do for themselves. I will try to be a person in the sense of a true individual, and a *personality* in the sense of a Selfless Person.

(b) 'Licence they mean when they cry liberty,' exclaimed the indignant Milton, commenting on the uproar occasioned by the publication of his *Tetrachordon*. Like 'liberty' itself, the word liberation is ambiguous, its meaning varying with the context within which it occurs and the kind of person to whom it refers. When we are told that 'western society is not a series of dangerous oppressions, but dangerous liberations,' we therefore have to ask what these liberations are, i.e. what they are liberations from, and what makes them dangerous. We also have to ask for whom they are liberations. (I leave aside the question of whether there in fact are no oppressions in Western society, or at least no dangerous ones.) Just as the self of whom we are thinking when we 'think of ourselves' may be either the group-member self or the true-individual self, so it may be either the group-member self or the true-individual self for whom liberations are liberations, and for whom they are dangerous. In the passage quoted by Mellor from Ajahn Sumedho's talk the liberations are from the constraints of the family, and since the self for whom they are liberations is the group-member self they are dangerous because they are individualistic. But in the case of the true-individual self liberations, whether from the family or anything else of a collective or group nature, are not dangerous because they are not individualistic. The danger is in the individualism, for as Milton goes on to insist, 'Who loves [liberty], must first be wise and good,' and wisdom and goodness are incompatible with individualism, whether in the seventeenth century or the twentieth. Hence although 'obsession with the individual' may indeed '[make] contemporary life "a neurotic and meaningless existence",' there is no doubt that a concern for true individuality, in oneself and in others, would transform contemporary or any other life into an existence that was psychologically healthy and spiritually meaningful.

For Mellor, if not for Ajahn Sumedho, liberty would appear to be a dirty word, possibly on account of its association with the French Revolution. But it is certainly not a dirty word for Buddhism. Principally in the form vimukti it occurs throughout the Buddhist scriptures, vimukti or liberation from the fetters of mundane existence being one of the key concepts of the Buddha's teaching. In a famous passage in the *Udāna* the Buddha, describing the eight ways in which the Dharma-Vinaya resembled the mighty ocean, declares that as the mighty ocean has one taste, the taste of salt, just so the Dharma-Vinaya has one taste, the taste of freedom or liberation (*vimukti*).[47] Besides being one of the four dharma-skandhas or 'parts of righteous living', vimukti constitutes the penultimate nidāna or 'link' of the positive and progressive 'spiral' aspect of conditioned co-origination (*pratītya-samutpāda*). It is also a synonym for

Nirvana. Hence it is not surprising that the concept of liberty, freedom, deliverance, or emancipation (as the word vimukti is variously translated) should feature prominently in the thinking of the FWBO or, for the matter of that, in the thinking of any Buddhist group, Western or non-Western. In my own expositions of the Dharma I usually connect vimukti with liberation from the first of the three fetters, as I do in *The Taste of Freedom*, with which Mellor appears not to be acquainted. Vimukti being the fourth 'positive and progressive' nidāna on from the crucial fifth nidāna, or 'knowledge-and-vision-of-things-as-they-really-are' (*yathābhūta-jñānadarśana*), there is, I point out, no real liberation without (transcendental) insight or 'clear vision' (*vipaśyanā*), and since it is insight or clear vision that breaks the first three fetters (as it does the remaining fetters) this means, in effect, that there is no real liberation without liberation from those first three fetters, i.e. from the fetter of speculative views regarding the self, the fetter of pathological doubt, and the fetter of attachment to moral rules and formal religious observances. All three fetters are therefore dealt with at some length in my writings and lectures, and a good deal of FWBO teaching and practice centres upon them.

Not that it is easy to break the first three fetters. Not that it is easy to achieve real liberation, thus becoming what is traditionally known as a Stream-Entrant. Before the first three fetters can be broken there are many minor liberations to be achieved, some of which Ajahn Sumedho and Mellor would doubtless regard as being no less dangerous, i.e. no less individualistic, than liberation from the constraints of the family. In the case of the true individual, however, such minor liberations are stepping-stones to the major liberations comprised in the breaking of the first three fetters or Stream-Entry. Though minor liberations may indeed be the immediate concern of individual members of the FWBO, it nevertheless is the major liberations that are, short of Buddhahood, their ultimate concern. They are concerned with minor liberations, whether social, psychological, cultural, or even religious, *because* they are concerned with the major liberations. This is not to say that one may not sometimes be deceived and think that he is behaving like a true individual when in fact he is behaving individualistically. Between true individuality at one end of the spectrum and individualism at the other there is a whole range of attitudes and it is not always easy to know what one's own position in the spectrum really is, especially if one does not have the support of spiritual friends. But this is the only *real* danger. To escape from the dangers of the minor liberations by giving up the minor liberations is not only to escape from individualism but also, at the same time, to give up the possibility of real individuality and therewith the possibility of ethical and spiritual life.

(c) The FWBO is an exceptionally individualistic movement. Because it is individualistic it is hostile to Christianity, which puts limits to individual development, and hostile to the family, because it does not allow the individual to think of himself. Moreover it is characterized by that obsession with the individual which according to Ajahn Sumedho makes contemporary life 'a neurotic and meaningless existence.'—Such is Mellor's estimate of the FWBO. Such is the estimate on which he bases his assertion that the difference between the English Sangha and the FWBO is rooted in competing understandings of history, with the English Sangha seeing itself as 'working against the grain of western culture' and the FWBO seeing itself as 'the pinnacle of a long evolutionary development.' How the English Sangha is related to Western culture, and how the FWBO is related to it, we shall see when we come to the next section of Mellor's article. Our present concern is with the question of whether the FWBO really does see itself as 'the pinnacle of a long evolutionary development'. Since the kind of context within which the FWBO views evolution has been touched on more than once already, in a general way, I can therefore be brief.

Real evolution is spiritual. Real evolution takes place when the group member or statistical individual becomes a true individual and when the true individual, upon the breaking of the first three fetters binding to mundane existence, becomes a Stream-Entrant and starts ascending, without possibility of regress, the successive stages of the transcendental Path whose final stage conducts into the presence of Nirvana. Thus real evolution is not evolution in the usual collective, biological sense, and does not form part of human history, except to the extent that the true individual interacts with the group and affects its life in various ways. I therefore sometimes distinguish between evolution, progress, and development. Evolution, in this context, is a strictly biological process, and corresponds to what in other contexts I term the Lower Evolution. Progress has reference to complexity of social organization and extent of scientific knowledge and technology. In itself it has no ethical or spiritual value, though it may provide the material and cultural basis for that which does have ethical or spiritual value. Development appertains to the individual, especially the true individual, and corresponds to what I also term the Higher Evolution. Such development has two successive stages, that from individuality through true individuality to Stream-Entry, and that from Stream-Entry to Enlightenment (*bodhi*) or Nirvana. If the FWBO was to see 'evolutionary development' as having a 'pinnacle' that pinnacle would not be the FWBO itself but the upper reaches of the higher evolutionary process, i.e. the purely transcendental second stage of development.

Within the confines of British Buddhism the FWBO sees itself as being a more adequate basis for the development of true individuality than were the Buddhist societies and Eastern Buddhist groups by which it was preceded and which continue, in some cases, to exist alongside it. But it does not see itself as being a more adequate basis simply because it is subsequent to them in time (this would amount to linear evolutionism) but because it has, as it believes, brought out more clearly than they have done the fundamental character of Buddhism, especially as consisting, so far as the individual Buddhist is concerned, in the act of Going for Refuge to the Three Jewels. This is not to say that it is wrong to regard the FWBO as being an advance on previous British Buddhist groups, as Mellor seems to think. It is an advance on them in much the same way that the Eastern Buddhist groups were an advance on the Buddhist societies, and the Buddhist societies themselves an advance on the scattering of scholarly knowledge about Buddhism by which *they* were preceded. If it is wrong to see in the FWBO an advance on the Eastern Buddhist groups, then it is no less wrong to see in the Buddhist societies an advance on the scattering of scholarly knowledge about Buddhism and no less wrong to see in *this* an advance on the British people's former total ignorance of the subject. But I would characterize all these advances as *progress*, not as evolution and not as, necessarily, development. Though in theory all, from the scattering of scholarly knowledge about Buddhism to the FWBO itself, may be bases for the arising of true individuality (insight or clear vision may on occasion be sparked off by a single line of Buddhist text), in practice true individuality is much more likely to arise on the basis of a movement such as the FWBO than on the basis of a scattering of scholarly knowledge about Buddhism. If British Buddhism's one hundred year history is the 'long evolutionary development' to which Mellor refers, then it *may* be correct to see the FWBO as the pinnacle of that development. Personally, however, I see the FWBO not so much as a pinnacle as a foundation, even a part of a foundation.

8 Consideration of the repercussions from the FWBO's modernism has led Mellor to the subject of tradition. This he now considers on its own, which in turn leads him to a consideration of the subject of charisma. Having observed that 'tradition' is not a fashionable concept in contemporary society, he turns for support to Edward Shils, one of the sociologist mentors whom we encountered in the first section of his article. According to Shils, while people may use the term 'tradition' in a variety of senses, there is a widespread rejection of tradition as a normative power, traditions as normative models of action and belief being regarded as useless and burdensome. 'Those who are attached to institutions, practices and beliefs which are designated as traditional are called "reactionaries" or rather "conservatives"; they are placed on the "right" on a line which runs from "left" to "right" and to be "on the right" is to be in the wrong.' Shils traces the origin of such a perspective to the (eighteenth century) Enlightenment which he sees as 'antithetical to tradition', a point which has been echoed, according to Mellor, by the ecclesiologist Joseph Ratzinger, in defence of the Catholic Church's tradition. 'Freedom emerges here [i.e. in the Enlightenment],' he quotes Ratzinger as saying, 'as liberation from the power of tradition to lay down norms.'

Unfortunately, though Shils can be relied on for support to a certain extent his position is not entirely satisfactory. He has, in fact, an ambivalent attitude to the Enlightenment. 'As a whole his book is in defence of the normative value of tradition,' Mellor complains, 'yet he applauds the Enlightenment for freeing the self from the "dark inheritance" of (Christian) tradition,' the ideal of the Enlightenment being (in Shils's words) 'to expunge from human beings all that came from the past and hindered their complete self-regulation and expression'. I am unable to refer to *Tradition* (it is out of print), but it is clear that for Shils belief, in principle, in the normative power of tradition is by no means incompatible with the rejection, in practice, of particular 'traditional' institutions, practices, or beliefs, which of course implies the existence of a criterion of what is really traditional and what is not. Whether Shils has such a criterion I do not know. Mellor certainly does not have one. It is clear that for him the question of distinguishing between what is really traditional and what is not simply does not arise, the normative power of tradition being definitely incompatible with the rejection of particular traditional institutions, practices, or beliefs. For Mellor tradition is tradition is tradition just as for Gertrude

Stein a rose is a rose is a rose. Tradition is something unitary, monolithic, absolute. Tradition is, in short, God, and rejection of tradition is rebellion against God.

So far as Mellor's quarrel with the FWBO is concerned, however, the difference with Shils is immaterial. Shils traces the rejection of the normative power of tradition to the Enlightenment and in the present context this is what matters. The FWBO, being individualistic, rejects tradition, and since it rejects tradition its attitude to Christianity bears a close resemblance to the 'achievement' of the Enlightenment (the inverted commas are Mellor's), i.e. to the Enlightenment's freeing of self from the 'dark inheritance' of (Christian) tradition. 'Subhuti asserts that the idea of sin "weakens the individual", disabling the attempt to regulate his own moral life or to develop spiritually. To fight these Christian "dangers for the individual" Subhuti stresses the necessity and value of blaspheming, ridiculing and developing contempt for God. The individual must be liberated from the past at all costs.' Needless to say, the individual who is weakened by the Christian idea of sin (very different from the Buddhist idea of akuśala-karma or 'unskilful action') is not the individualist but the true individual, or at least the nascent true individual. Again, Mellor is unable to imagine a state of affairs in which group and (true) individual are in conflict and unable, therefore, to understand that there are traditions which, since they weaken (true) individuality or even discourage its emergence altogether, have to be rejected if (true) individuality is to be developed. But there is no need for me to labour the point, as Mellor's confusion should by now be obvious. The nature of the 'therapeutic blasphemy' (as I term it) of which Subhuti speaks is explained in my *Buddhism and Blasphemy*, which Mellor appears not to have come across. As for the individual having to be liberated from the past 'at all costs', does not the Buddha say, in the *Dhammapada*, 'Give up the future, *give up the past*, give up the present, and pass to the Farther Shore (i.e. Nirvana)'?[48]

9 But Mellor has not yet finished with the (eighteenth century) Enlightenment. Continuity with Enlightenment discourse is of significance not only for the rejection (in the case of the FWBO) of the normative power of tradition but also for the legitimation of authority in 'English' Buddhism. Following, as he tells us, Max Weber's distinction of 'traditional authority' and 'charismatic authority', Mellor argues that the English Sangha conforms to a model of traditional authority in that it understands itself to be an organic development of Thai forest monasticism. 'Ajahn Sumedho trained with Ajahn Chah (who had himself trained with figures such as Ajahn Mun), giving the English Sangha an impeccable traditional pedigree, and therefore authority. The FWBO, on the other hand, is more akin to a model of charismatic authority, in that Sangharakshita distinguishes between what he regards as "essentially" Buddhism and mere "traditions", in the sense of cultural customs.' At this point Mellor quotes me as saying, in my 1986 interview with him:

'I distinguish between Tradition with a capital T and tradition with a small T. By tradition with a small T I mean those observances, customs, practices, which have become traditional in Buddhist countries but are quite peripheral in relation to the fundamental principles of Buddhist teachings.... I think that at present the Thai-trained Sangha Trust people [i.e. the English Sangha, the members of which are supported by the Sangha Trust] tend to look at tradition in that way, whereas I think of Tradition in the sense of the essential principles of Buddhism.'

According to Mellor, 'This is a charismatic model of authority because Sangharakshita is understood to have the personal authority to be able to distinguish between what is, and is not, essential Buddhism.'

Valid though Weber's distinction between traditional authority and charismatic authority may be, it is not so absolute as Mellor thinks, nor so applicable to contemporary 'English' Buddhism. What he says about the English Sangha and what he says about the FWBO could quite easily be transposed. 'The FWBO', it could be said, 'conforms to a model of traditional authority in that it understands itself to be an organic development of Indo-Tibetan Triyana Buddhism: Sangharakshita trained with Dhardo Rimpoche (who himself trained with such figures as Geshe Yeshe Lhundup), as well as with other Indian, Tibetan, and Chinese teachers, giving the FWBO an impeccable traditional pedigree, and therefore authority. The English Sangha, on the other hand, is more akin to a model of charismatic authority, in that Ajahn Chah, Ajahn Sumedho's teacher, distinguishes between what in Buddhism needs to be purified and what does not.' (Earlier in the section Mellor describes Ajahn Chah as 'using tradition to purify tradition'.) 'This is a charismatic model of authority because Ajahn Chah is understood to have the personal authority to be able to distinguish between what in Buddhism needs to be purified and what does not.' Thus whether one distinguishes between Tradition with a capital T and tradition with a small T, or between what in Buddhism needs to be purified and what does not, makes little difference. In either case, the fact that one distinguishes means that one has a criterion, a criterion implies a definition, whether of 'tradition' or of 'purity', and a definition implies essence (*vide supra*, p.47 *et seq.*). As Mellor perceives, 'What the FWBO understands by "Tradition" is *essence*; that is, the heart and core of Buddhism when shorn of all cultural accretions.' What he is unable to perceive is that the statement could be transposed, and that he could equally well say, 'What the Thai forest tradition understands by "Pure Buddhism" is *essence*; that is, the heart and core of Buddhism when shorn of all impure elements.' My 'Tradition' with a capital T thus corresponds in principle to Ajahn Chah's (and presumably the English Sangha's) 'Pure Buddhism' and my tradition with a small T or cultural accretions to Ajahn Chah's impure elements or what in Buddhism is in need of purification. It would therefore not be surprising if in applying our respective criteria to particular Buddhist customs and beliefs we should sometimes come to similar conclusions about them. An example will make this clear.

According to an article in the *Bangkok Post*, there are between 500,000 and 1,000,000 prostitutes in Thailand, a significant number of whom are 'eldest daughters who, according to tradition, are expected to sacrifice for the families' common welfare in time of need.' In many villages, monks are drawn into the procurement process. 'Procurers will come to the temples as hosts of the forest robe offering ceremony. The monks will recruit young girls to serve food and drinks during the event as part of the village's hospitality. The temple has become the ground to select girls for the next batch.' Moreover, monks often say that a woman becomes a prostitute because of bad deeds in past lives and that 'sins can be diluted by making merits by giving money to the temples,' with the result that, 'It is common to find temples in the home villages of prostitutes beautifully decorated from these girls' donations.'[49] Thailand is of course a Buddhist country, its monks are Buddhist monks, and the 500,000 to 1,000,000 prostitutes are Buddhist prostitutes. The tradition that eldest daughters become prostitutes in time of need, that monks take part in the procurement process, and that prostitutes dilute their sins by 'making merits' by giving money to the temples, are therefore *Buddhist* traditions and form part of Thai Buddhism. The FWBO would maintain, however, that they are traditions with a small T, not Tradition with a capital T, and that being in fact cultural accretions they are quite peripheral to the fundamental principles of Buddhism. In terms of my earlier analysis, a Buddhist essence is present in them only to a very limited degree, if at all (*vide supra*, p.48). Ajahn Chah, I imagine, would be of a similar opinion, as would Ajahn Sumedho and the English Sangha. He would no doubt take the view that the traditions in question were, in his own terms, impure elements or part of what in Buddhism needs to be purified. What view

Mellor would take I do not know. For him religions have only a social and cultural existence, and inasmuch as he does not distinguish between horizontally transpersonal and vertically transpersonal social forms there are, for him, no such things as cultural accretions or impure elements and nothing, therefore, that needs to be shorn away. Perhaps he would take the view that the prostitutes of Thailand should simply carry on 'making merits'. After all, to reject tradition would be individualistic.

Be that as it may, Mellor not only perceives that 'What the FWBO understands as "Tradition" is *essence*'; he also sees this as establishing a continuity with (eighteenth century) Enlightenment discourse. That for the FWBO Tradition = essence is significant because 'it highlights how the FWBO shares in the Enlightenment's antipathy to tradition, even when it uses the word positively in its own discourse.' It highlights no such thing. Any 'antipathy' the FWBO may feel relates to such traditions as eldest daughters becoming prostitutes in time of need, monks taking part in the procurement process, and prostitutes diluting their sins by 'making merits' by giving money to the temples, and has a basis very different from the more individualistic basis of the Enlightenment's antipathy to tradition, the basis of the FWBO's antipathy being simply the obverse of its sympathy with and concern for the true individual or individual-in-relation-to-Buddhahood. As for the FWBO's positive use of the term tradition in its own discourse, this is not inconsistent with its antipathy to tradition, as Mellor seems to think, since the tradition to which the FWBO is antipathetic is tradition with a small T, whereas the term it uses positively in its discourse is Tradition with a capital T. It is therefore *not* clear that 'To use Shils's terms ... the FWBO would place itself on the "left" of the line first drawn in the Enlightenment which runs from "left" to "right",' as Mellor goes on to assert. Far from this being clear, it should be evident from my previous explanations that the FWBO would no more place itself on the left of such a line than would the English Sangha. Indeed, it would not place itself in any relation to it at all, its preoccupations being of an entirely different order. Hence there can be no question of a reason for its so placing itself, and therefore no question of that reason being that 'they are not interested in the operation of traditions which they regard as "reactionary".' Quite apart from the fact that the only traditions the FWBO regards as reactionary (a term it does not actually use) are traditions with a small T, it is certainly interested in the 'operation' of such (reactionary) traditions, if only because these are inimical to the development of (true) individuality and their influence has to be counteracted.

From the charismatic model of authority Mellor passes to the meaning of charisma in recent history. But before we follow him there I want to backtrack a little and (a) look at the notion of personal authority and (b) correct what may appear to be an inconsistency on my part with regard to the English Sangha.

(a) According to Mellor, the FWBO is more akin to a model of charismatic authority because Sangharakshita is understood to have the personal authority to be able to distinguish between what is, and what is not, essential Buddhism. But what is this 'personal authority'? In what does it consist? Whence is it derived? I would say (and I think I have a voice in the matter) that it is not a question of first having the personal (i.e. charismatic) authority and then, because one has that authority, being somehow able to distinguish between what is, and what is not, essential Buddhism. Mellor puts the cart before the horse. It is really the other way round. First one becomes able, by virtue of study and meditation, to distinguish between what is essential Buddhism, and what is not, and then one is understood as having personal authority because, appealing to their reason and experience, one enables people to see the difference for themselves. The Buddha himself conforms to this 'charismatic' model of authority, as do all the great spiritual masters who were founders of schools. There is no question of their authority having its source in ecclesiastical position or political power, or in the supernatural in the Judaeo-Christian sense. There is not even any question of its having its source in tradition, in that tradition does not exist in the abstract, as it were, but only as embodied in individuals, so that even 'traditional' authority is *spiritually* efficacious only to the extent that it is mediated by 'charismatic' individuals.

(b) I have shown that whatever Mellor says about the English Sangha and the FWBO, regarding their being authority models and regarding the matter of 'essence', can quite easily be transposed. I have also shown that *in principle* there is no difference between my rejection of cultural accretions to Buddhism and Ajahn Chah's purging tradition of impure elements. In the passage Mellor quotes from my interview with him, however, I describe the English Sangha as tending to see tradition as those observances, customs, and practices which, though they have become traditional in Buddhist countries, are quite peripheral in relation to the fundamental principles of Buddhism. The inconsistency is due to the fact that in order to show how Ajahn Chah and I, applying our respective criteria to particular Buddhist customs and beliefs, could come to similar conclusions about them, I deliberately chose an extreme example of such customs and beliefs, that of the Thai Buddhist prostitutes. The example had to be an extreme one so that there could be no doubt that Ajahn Chah and I *would* come to similar conclusions about it and no doubt, therefore, that we were *in principle* agreed that it was possible to reject cultural accretions, as I would say, or to purge impure elements, as he would say, even though these had become traditional in Buddhist countries—a possibility that for Mellor does not exist. That Ajahn Chah and I are agreed in principle does not necessarily mean that we always agree in practice, and indeed such is certainly not the case. Much that for me belongs to tradition with a small T for him is part of Tradition with a capital T, and probably this is the case to an even greater extent where the English Sangha is concerned. As Mellor observes in connection with the question of ritual, 'For the English

Sangha, the Thai forest tradition is an absolute standard by which the tradition in England must be judged, so that discipline, hierarchy, doctrine and ritual observance are followed as strictly as possible in the west,' and it is for this reason that in the passage from my interview I describe the English Sangha as tending, at present, to see tradition in terms of observances, customs, and practices which, though peripheral to the fundamental principles of Buddhism, have become traditional in Buddhist countries. But even the English Sangha would, I am sure, agree in principle that it was possible to distinguish between Tradition with a capital T and tradition with a small T. If pressed, I suspect they would admit that the Thai forest tradition itself was not entirely free from cultural accretions, though it was not yet feasible to discard them.

That Ajahn Chah and I, while being agreed in principle, should differ considerably in practice, is hardly surprising. Differences with regard to tradition with a small T are to be found not only between different schools of Buddhism but also within the individual schools themselves. As I pointed out in my interview with Mellor, in the words represented in his quotation by a row of dots, some Theravada monks consider it important to cover both shoulders with the upper robe when going for alms while others do not. The latter adhere to their own traditions (with a small T), regarding *them* as being of importance. I did not believe, I added, that it was important to maintain differences of this sort in the West, even if it was possible to decide which traditions with a small T one was going to perpetuate. Since then I have heard that there is a difference of opinion within the English Sangha with regard to the 'white cloth'. This is a piece of fabric on which the Theravada monks of Thailand (though not those of Sri Lanka, Burma, Laos, and Cambodia) receive offerings from women, so as not to come into physical contact with them as they make their offerings. Some members of the English Sangha believe that it is important to perpetuate this tradition in the West, while others do not, though for the time being all continue to adhere to it.

10 The present section of Mellor's article is the longest, and my
response to it has been long in proportion. He does not conclude
it, however, without a parting shot at the FWBO's alleged antipathy to tradition (he continues, of course, to ignore my distinction between Tradition with a capital T and tradition with a
small T). But if Mellor fires the shot, it is Sennett who loads the
gun. Sennett draws attention, so Mellor tells us, to the modification of the meaning of charisma in recent history. 'He stresses
that charisma in a Roman Catholic context has referred to something quite impersonal.... In contrast, the modern, secular understanding of charisma has come to refer to a forceful
personality so that the public space, the trans-personal objectivity, of the Catholic doctrine has been lost.' For Mellor,
Sennett's emphasis on the rational, personalistic character of this
change, recalls both Shils's and Ratzinger's understandings of
the radical outlook of the (eighteenth century) Enlightenment,
secular charisma being, in Sennett's words, 'a rational way to
think about politics in a culture ruled by belief in the immanent
... rejecting as hypothetical, mystical or "pre-modern" belief in
that which cannot be directly experienced. You can directly feel
a politician's sentiments; you cannot directly feel the future consequences of his policies.'

Presumably Sennett refers to the politician because he possesses 'secular charisma'. However that may be, Mellor hastens to
assure us that 'Sangharakshita is not a politician so any parallel
must be treated cautiously.' Having covered his back, so to
speak, in this way, he proceeds to assert that the antipathy
manifested in the appeal to a trans-historical essence (i.e. the
FWBO's appeal), and the location of religious significance in the
person (i.e. the FWBO's alleged location of it there) suggests a
continuity with the sort of trend Sennett is describing. Thus a
connection is established between secular charisma and the Enlightenment, and between the FWBO as represented by its

founder and secular charisma, and Mellor is able to reiterate his charges that the FWBO is personalistic, liberationist, 'clearly modernistic' in its 'characterization of history', and individualistic. To crown all, the FWBO envisages tradition as 'a reactionary brake on the historical drive to liberation'. Since I have dealt with these misunderstandings and misrepresentations already I need say nothing about them now. There is, however, one new charge, to the effect that 'When the FWBO looks at the religious and cultural traditions of the west (and often of the east), they do not see Sennett's "civilized" tolerance of "human frailty", but enemies of the individual.' I shall take a look at this new charge. But first a few words about charisma.

For Mellor I have charismatic authority, rather than traditional authority, in that I am understood to have the personal authority to be able to distinguish between what is, and what is not, essential to Buddhism. Since he regards me as having charismatic authority, and since that authority is personal, he obviously sees me as being possessed by charisma of some kind. But of *what* kind? Certainly not of the 'impersonal' Roman Catholic kind, in the sense of the 'gift of grace' which, according to Sennett (as quoted by Mellor), enters into the priest when he utters the holy words, so that the rituals he performs have meaning no matter what the (ethical and spiritual) state of his person. The other kind of charisma is that of the 'forceful personality' as exemplified by the politician, but Mellor is aware that I am not a politician and that any parallel between the politician's capacity to influence people and mine must be treated cautiously. Thus although he sees me as being possessed of charisma he is unable to say what kind of charisma I possess. This is not surprising. As I point out in connection with the charismatic model of authority (*vide supra*, p.131), it is not a question of my having charismatic authority and then, because I have charismatic authority, being somehow able to distinguish between what is, and what is not, Buddhism. All I have is the ability distinguish between what is, and what is not, Buddhism.

Thus the fact that I have 'charismatic authority' does not mean that I have charisma. The truth of the matter is that I have never regarded myself as possessing charisma (in the popular sense), and have always been suspicious of it in others. Adapting the French poet's well known line, I once told a seminar, 'Take charisma and wring its neck.' Charisma is to person what rhetoric is to speech, which is why I sometimes refer to charisma as 'the rhetoric of the person'. Rhetoric is the art of inducing people to accept what you say because they like the way you say it. Similarly, charisma is the trick of getting people to respond positively to what you stand for, or what you represent, simply because they respond positively to you, or what they think is you. Charisma thus tends to obliterate the vital distinction between reliance on a person (*pudgala-pratiśaraṇā*), as Buddhism terms it, and reliance on truth or reality (*dharma-pratiśaraṇa*), and it is for this reason that communication of the Dharma by means of charisma is not encouraged in the FWBO. The only kind of 'charisma' that is encouraged is that of enabling people to understand and practise the Dharma by appealing to their reason and experience.

The notion of civilized tolerance of human frailty comes from Sennett's emphasis on the impersonality of the Roman Catholic doctrine of charisma, according to which the 'gift of grace' entered into the priest, when he uttered the holy words, so that the rituals he performed had meaning no matter what the state of his person. 'The doctrine of charisma was eminently civilized,' continues Sennett (as quoted by Mellor), 'it was tolerant of human frailty at the same time it proclaimed the supremacy of religious truth.' How Mellor can say, 'When the FWBO looks at the religious and cultural traditions of the west (and often of the east), they do not see Sennett's "civilized" tolerance of "human frailty", but enemies of the individual' is far from clear. The frailty of which the Roman Catholic doctrine of charisma is tolerant, in the passage quoted, is the frailty of the priest, whose person was so likely to be in a state of sin that, as the Church

was quick to realize, unless the rituals he performed were meaningful (i.e. efficacious, in the sense of being channels of divine
grace) independently of the state of his person there could be no
meaningful rituals. What Subhuti attacks as enemies of the individual, in the passage of *Buddhism for Today* to which Mellor's
note refers us, are the nuclear family, Christianity, and pseudo-
liberalism. Whether these really exhibit the same kind of 'frailty'
as the priest and therefore whether 'tolerance' of that frailty is
really a 'civilized' tolerance of *human* frailty is doubtful.
Tolerance of human frailty is a very different thing from pander-
ing to human weakness, and we pander to that weakness when
we fail to attack religious and cultural traditions that are
enemies of the individual in that they hinder the development
of the (true) individual or individual-in-relation-to-
Buddhahood. Such 'tolerance' is not tolerance but betrayal. True
tolerance of human weakness is an expression of compassion,
and I hope the FWBO harkens to the voice of compassion. In
what Sennett and Mellor have to say about the Roman Catholic
doctrine of charisma, and about civilized tolerance of human
frailty, I do not hear the voice of compassion. Rather do I hear
the insidious accents of Dostoyevsky's Grand Inquisitor.

MELLOR DOES NOT define culture, any more than he defines Protestantism, or modernism, or tradition, or any of the other key terms in his discourse (though he does list some of the major characteristics of *liberal* Protestantism), and it is therefore difficult to know the sort of idea of culture he has at the back of his mind when he considers the FWBO's and the English Sangha's particular understandings of the relationship between religion and culture. At the back of my own mind, as I protest some of Mellor's assertions about the FWBO and affirm its and my own attitudes, will be an idea of culture as discussed by Arnold, Eliot, and Steiner, as well as an awareness of the word's 'complexity of idea and reference', in Raymond Williams's phrase.[50] Not that I intend bringing that classic discussion of theirs, or any part of it, to bear on the questions ventilated by Mellor in this section of his article. Though I have long wanted to write systematically on the relationship between Buddhism and culture, a topic that has preoccupied me for almost as long as I have been a Buddhist, this is not the place for any move in that direction, the more especially since this 'response' of mine is already much longer than originally planned. Instead, I shall confine myself to commenting on Mellor's misunderstandings and misrepresentations of the FWBO's (and my own) position with regard to such issues as the separateness of Buddhism and culture, the idea of 'born Buddhists', and 'exoticism', without entering into issues of a more general nature, and without going over ground that has not been gone over already in connection with other issues.

1 'For both the FWBO and the English Sangha culture and

religion are quite separate, although the ways in which this view is expressed vary considerably.' Having given us this information, which may well be true, Mellor proceeds, with the help of one of his sociologist mentors, to the most flagrant of his many misrepresentations of the FWBO. The mentor in question is Neusner, who argues, 'as noted earlier', that the Protestant location of religious significance in the individual makes religion a 'constituent of conscience' rather than a 'component of culture'. According to Mellor, 'The FWBO displays this understanding of religion and culture,' from which it follows that for the FWBO, 'one can be a Buddhist regardless of culture, adherence to traditional Buddhist disciplines and rituals, or even knowledge of Buddhist doctrine.' The first time I read this extraordinary statement it took my breath away. If from the FWBO's understanding of religion and culture it follows that one can be a Buddhist regardless of culture, adherence to traditional Buddhist disciplines and rituals, or even knowledge of Buddhist doctrine, then why is it that the FWBO's 450 Order members and 1,000 Mitras are found observing the Precepts, meditating, performing pujas, studying Buddhist texts, both canonical and noncanonical, practising Right or Perfect Livelihood, and celebrating Buddhist festivals? Why is it that I have been teaching meditation, leading pujas, and expounding Buddhist doctrine in the West for the last twenty-five years? Why is it that I am now concerning myself with misunderstandings and misrepresentations of the FWBO and, indeed, of the Dharma itself?

Mellor's present misrepresentation is based on his failure to understand the FWBO's (fully traditional) teaching on Going for Refuge. 'Sangharakshita rejects the idea of "born Buddhists", people who are "Buddhist" by virtue of being born into a Buddhist culture.' This is true, except that I would say '*merely* by virtue of being born into a Buddhist culture', and should be understood as saying this when we come to consider the idea of 'born Buddhists' later on. '[For Sangharakshita] becoming a Buddhist is a faith-decision, a "conversion", a personal decision to "go for refuge".' I have indeed spoken of becoming a Buddhist as a conversion, and once gave a series of four lectures on 'The Meaning of Conversion in Buddhism', but I have never spoken of becoming a Buddhist as a faith-decision. Indeed, the term is quite new to me, and in applying it, without explanation, to the act of Going for Refuge, Mellor not only again violates an elementary rule of methodology but also compounds his failure to understand the FWBO's teaching on Going for Refuge by the introduction of an element of ambiguity. Is a faith-decision a decision *about* faith, in the sense of its being a decision as to the acceptance of a particular form of religious belief, or is it a decision that is the *result* of faith, in the sense of its being a decision made in consequence of adherence to a particular form of religious belief? Whichever it may be, Mellor evidently believes that 'a personal decision to "go for refuge",' on the one hand, and culture, adherence to traditional Buddhist disciplines, and knowledge of Buddhist doctrine, on the other, are incompatible, or at least distinct and separable. This implies a very superficial understanding of Going for Refuge. As explained in *The History of My Going for Refuge*, to which Mellor refers us at this point, but which he appears not to have actually read, there are four levels of Going for Refuge, broadly speaking: provisional, effective, real, and absolute. Provisional Going for Refuge (which includes cultural and ethnic, or merely formal, Going for Refuge) is that which is tentative and partial. In the FWBO this level is represented by the Mitra. Effective Going for Refuge is that which involves the individual's whole conscious being, and in which the Three Jewels are placed at the centre of the mandala of one's personal existence. This level is represented by the Order member, the 'effectiveness' of whose Going for Refuge receives formal (though not merely formal) recognition at the time of his or her ordination. Real Going for Refuge is that which takes place when one develops insight and wisdom, thereby entering upon the transcendental Path. This level is synonymous with Stream-Entry and the Opening of the

Dharma Eye. Absolute Going for Refuge is that of the Buddha, who is his own refuge.[51] Far from Going for Refuge being incompatible with, or at least distinct and separable from, culture, adherence to traditional Buddhist disciplines, and knowledge of Buddhist doctrine, as Mellor believes, the latter are for the FWBO the very means by which Order members seek to transform their effective but still mundane Going for Refuge into real or transcendental Going for Refuge. Thus to assert that according to the FWBO 'one can be a Buddhist regardless of culture, adherence to traditional Buddhist disciplines and rituals, or even knowledge of Buddhist doctrine,' is a misrepresentation of the most glaring kind.

Mellor is able to misrepresent the FWBO in this way, not just by ignoring facts, but also by means of the sleight of hand by which he links 'culture' with 'adherence to traditional Buddhist disciplines' and 'knowledge of Buddhist doctrine'. Since for the FWBO culture and religion are, according to Mellor, quite separate, it follows that for the FWBO adherence to traditional Buddhist disciplines and rituals and knowledge of Buddhist doctrine, on the one hand, and religion (i.e. religion as a 'constituent of conscience'), on the other, are quite separate too. For the FWBO, therefore, it is possible to be a Buddhist regardless of culture, adherence to traditional Buddhist disciplines and rituals, or even knowledge of Buddhist doctrine. Moreover, Sangharakshita's rejection of the idea of 'born Buddhists' means that 'becoming a Buddhist is a faith-decision, a "conversion", a personal decision to "go for refuge",' and a faith-decision, Mellor evidently thinks, is something that takes place in an ethical and intellectual vacuum. Nor is this all. Since for the FWBO culture and religion are 'quite separate', it also follows that for the FWBO culture is of very little significance and value. 'Even when the FWBO refers to culture in a positive sense,' Mellor charges, 'e.g. the creation of a new western Buddhist culture, it understands it as merely a beneficial offshoot of "spiritually-aware" individuals which, in turn, helps individuals to "grow".'

Though we are referred here to *Buddhism for Today*, p.129, Mellor in fact is not even paraphrasing Subhuti who, despite the inverted commas, makes no mention of 'spiritually-aware' individuals, either on the page in question or in the rest of the chapter. But we have grown accustomed to Mellor's rather cavalier treatment of his sources, and there is no need for me to dwell on the matter. Let us hear the rest of his charge against the FWBO's understanding of culture. 'Any possible autonomy of culture is severely restricted by the FWBO's hostility to the idea of the "group": all collective, supra-individual structures are the objects of suspicion precisely because religious significance is located so exclusively within the individual. Even the idea of the Sangha is firmly differentiated from anything suggestive of a "group".' Here we are again referred to *Buddhism for Today*, this time to p.131, and this time with some justification, and Mellor concludes his present charge against the FWBO by returning to a favourite theme. 'The FWBO's attitude to the relationship between religion and culture,' he declares, 'underlines its individualistic orientation.'

I have already shown that there is a difference between (true) individuality and individualism, and that the FWBO's emphasis on the development of the true individual, or individual-in-relation-to-Buddhahood, is *not* evidence of an individualistic orientation on its part. I have also shown that there is a difference between *horizontally* transpersonal social forms (or 'collective, supra-individual structures,' as Mellor now decides to call them) and *vertically* transpersonal forms, and a difference, therefore, between rejection of the one and rejection of the other. Finally (so far as Mellor's charge against the FWBO's understanding of culture is concerned), I have shown that for the FWBO religious significance is located not exclusively within the individual but within the (true) individual *and* the spiritual community, the individual himself being both subject and object, soul and citizen. These more basic misunderstandings and misrepresentations having been dealt with, it only remains for me to take Mellor up on his references to (a) culture as 'merely a beneficial offshoot', (b) the creation of a new western Buddhist culture, (c) the autonomy of culture, and (d) the idea of the Sangha.

(a) It is interesting that 'Even when the FWBO refers to culture in a positive sense ... it understands it as merely a beneficial offshoot of "spiritually-aware" individuals which, in turn, helps individuals to "grow".' *Merely*? Ignoring the suggestion that for the FWBO 'culture' is usually a grubby word, what *more* (it might be asked) could be said of a phenomenon that for the FWBO is 'a beneficial offshoot' (in Mellor's minimizing phrase) than that, as the 'collective' creation of a community of spiritually-aware individuals, it performs the invaluable function of supporting the efforts of the individual-to-be, as Subhuti calls him, to develop into a true individual and eventually enter upon the transcendental Path? Short of the transcendental Path itself, one could hardly imagine anything greater or more glorious than such a culture. Yet for Mellor it is 'merely' a beneficial offshoot—presumably because it only 'helps individuals to "grow",' a process that for him has decidedly individualistic connotations. Individuals ought to be content just to follow tradition.

(b) I am not being pedantic, I hope, in pointing out that when Mellor speaks of the FWBO as referring to 'the creation of a new western Buddhist culture' what he means to say is 'a new, western Buddhist culture'. There is no *old* western Buddhist culture for a new western Buddhist culture to supersede. At present Western Buddhism has no culture of its own, though the FWBO has taken a few very tentative steps in this direction, as have other Western Buddhist groups, particularly in the United States. Western Buddhism exists within a context of non-Buddhist culture. In this non-Buddhist and, in effect, often anti-Buddhist culture, it is possible to distinguish three strands or three components: folk culture, high culture, and mass culture. A distinctively Western Buddhist culture, when it emerges, will probably have three main sources. It will be the product of (i) the interaction between Western Buddhists and the traditional Eastern Buddhist cultures, especially as represented by their literature and fine arts, (ii) the interaction between Western Buddhists and elements of Western folk and high culture (though not, I think, mass culture, now rapidly becoming world-wide), and (iii) the inspiration Western Buddhists derive from their personal experience of the Dharma, especially their experience of meditation. Once this Western Buddhist culture has come into existence, a process that will take centuries rather than decades, it will function as a support for the individual Buddhist's practice of the Dharma, instead of functioning, as so much of our culture does today, as an obstacle and a hindrance. Until then we have no alternative but to create, within Western culture, pockets of more or less (Western) Buddhist culture within which the individual Buddhist may find, to some extent at least, that support for his practice of the Dharma which is so lacking in the outside world. It is with such an end in view that the FWBO has established, and continues to expand, that network of centres, communities, and team-based Right Livelihood businesses which constitute the nucleus of what it calls the New Society or, in more traditional terms, the Kingdom of the Dharma.

(c) 'Any possible autonomy of culture is severely restricted by the FWBO's hostility to the idea of the "group",' says Mellor, 'all collective, supra-individual structures [being] the objects of suspicion precisely because religious significance is located so exclusively within the individual.' We know that for the FWBO religious significance is *not* located exclusively within the individual, and we know that not all collective, supra-individual structures or transpersonal social forms are *vertically* transpersonal; but what is this 'autonomy of culture' which is said to be severely restricted by the FWBO's hostility to the idea of the 'group'? Mellor does not explain. Had one encountered the phrase in certain other contexts one would have assumed it referred to the idea that culture should be independent of religion, or even to the doctrine of 'art for art's sake', but in the present context such an assumption must be ruled out. Mellor would appear to believe that culture is identical with religion, just as society is identical with culture, the whole being, of course, 'transpersonal'. The only meaning I am therefore able to extract from his assertion that 'Any possible autonomy of culture is severely restricted by the FWBO's hostility to the "group",' is to the effect that the FWBO is wrong in thinking that spiritually-aware individuals should exercise an influence on the group. For Mellor the individual, whether spiritually-aware or not, has no autonomy. Autonomy is the prerogative of the group, as represented by religion, or culture, or society, or tradition. Thus the individual is swallowed up in Leviathan. All else is individualism.

(d) Just as the FWBO's attitude towards the group really is one of 'hostility' (though it is not a hostility that extends to the positive group), so its idea of the Sangha really is 'firmly differentiated' from anything suggestive of a group. Speaking of the latter, however, Mellor says, 'Even the idea of the Sangha' is differentiated in this way. *Even*? Again the adverb is significant, suggesting as it does, in this case, that for Mellor the Sangha or spiritual community, the transcendental counterpart of which is the Ārya Sangha, is in fact no more than the group *par excellence*. No wonder, then, that he should see the FWBO's attitude to the relationship between religion and culture as underlining its 'individualistic orientation'. So extreme is the FWBO's individualism, it would appear, that it is prepared to differentiate from anything suggestive of a 'group' even the idea of something as undeniably group-like in character as the Sangha.

2 For Mellor it must be a relief to be able to turn from the FWBO's attitude to the relationship between religion and culture, underlined as this is by its 'individualistic orientation', to the English Sangha's 'more sophisticated' understanding of that relationship. 'Unlike Sangharakshita', he tells us, 'Ajahn Sumedho attributes some significance to traditionally Buddhist cultures, regardless of individual faith-decisions.' Whether Ajahn Sumedho himself, in the interview from which Mellor proceeds to quote, actually speaks of 'faith-decisions' is not clear (I am inclined to think he does not), but perhaps this is irrelevant, except as possibly furnishing us with yet another example of Mellor's propensity to violate the elementary rules of methodology. The Ajahn begins by making the point that Asian teachers have been raised in a society that thinks and lives Buddhism—a point with which it is possible to agree, provided one does not take too close a look at what 'thinks and lives Buddhism' actually means. 'Whether they are devout or not does not make any difference. Nevertheless, it affects their whole outlook on themselves and the world.' Whether 'they' refers to the society that thinks and lives Buddhism or to the Asian teachers who have been raised in the society, is not clear. However, it is evident that Ajahn Sumedho does attribute 'some significance' to traditionally Buddhist cultures, and he concludes (at least so far as Mellor's quotation is concerned) by addressing his interviewer directly, and saying, 'Whereas you [unlike them] come from a culture which is materialistic, and where the values—based on greed and competition, and trust and faith in conceptual learning—have affected our mind.'

Mellor comments that as Ajahn Sumedho pictures things, 'the Buddhist has the support of culture in the east, but has to fight against it in the west.' This is broadly true, and I have no wish to underestimate the importance of the support a Buddhist culture is capable of giving to an individual's practice of the Dharma (it is because it does *not* underestimate the importance of such support that the FWBO seeks to create the nucleus of a New Society, or Kingdom of the Dharma). But Mellor's further comments on Ajahn Sumedho's 'more sophisticated' understanding of the relationship between religion and culture only serve to highlight the really dreadful confusion that lies at the heart of that understanding. 'In the east one can be a "Buddhist" whether one is devout or not, whereas in the west there is, perhaps, more of a need to be devout, since being a Buddhist is not a natural option.' According to Mellor, 'This brings Ajahn Sumedho close to Sangharakshita's recognition of the significance of the faith-decision for the Buddhist. Such a faith-decision may be a significant factor in an English context because of the persistence of Protestant orientations, even when it is not formalized into a doctrinal position as in the case of the FWBO.'

Whether Ajahn Sumedho has really been brought closer to Sangharakshita's 'recognition of the significance of the faith-decision for the Buddhist' it is difficult to say, the categories in which Mellor's comment is formulated probably being as foreign to the Ajahn as they are to me. For the same reason it is difficult to say whether such a faith-decision may be a significant factor in an English context and difficult, therefore, to say whether this is because of the persistence of Protestant orientations. In any case, I have shown that the FWBO, at least, is far from demonstrating what Mellor elsewhere calls 'continuities with Protestant perspectives' and therefore need not concern myself further with this particular misrepresentation. Let me proceed directly to the dreadful confusion, as I have termed it, that lies at the heart of Ajahn Sumedho's supposedly 'more sophisticated' understanding of the relationship between religion and culture. In so doing I shall, of course, be dealing with that confusion as represented by the quotation from Ajahn Sumedho's interview as utilized by Mellor for the purpose of comparing the English Sangha with the FWBO.

The confusion really is a dreadful one. Ajahn Sumedho appears to distinguish between 'thinking and living Buddhism', on the one hand, and 'being devout', on the other. But what does 'being devout' mean, especially as distinguished from 'thinking and living Buddhism'? In view of Mellor's comment that 'in the east one can be a "Buddhist" whether one is devout or not, whereas in the west there is, perhaps, more of a need to be devout' (a comment made, presumably, in the light of the interview as a whole), it would seem 'being devout' means actually practising Buddhism. Thus when Ajahn Sumedho distinguishes between 'thinking and living Buddhism' and 'being devout' he is in fact distinguishing between not practising Buddhism and practising it, which means that he identifies 'thinking and living Buddhism' with not practising Buddhism. No doubt this is why he goes on to say, 'Whether they [i.e. either the Asian teachers or the society in which they have been raised] are devout or not does not make any difference.' In other words, it does not make any difference whether one is devout or whether one thinks and lives Buddhism, that is, whether one practises Buddhism or does not practise it. 'Nevertheless,' the Ajahn adds, 'it affects their whole outlook on themselves and the world.' What affects it? Is it the fact that 'they' have been raised in a society that thinks and lives Buddhism (i.e. does not actually practise it), or is it the fact that it does not make any difference whether they are devout or not (i.e. practise Buddhism or do not practise it)? We are not told. Mellor's 'more sophisticated understanding' would appear to be indistinguishable from nonsense.

In order to extricate ourselves from the confusion we must go back to the statement, 'Whether they [i.e. either the Asian teachers or the society which they have been raised] are devout or not does not make any difference.' Does not make any difference to what? Obviously Ajahn Sumedho does not believe it makes no difference, ethically or spiritually, whether one practises Buddhism or not, since otherwise he would not have felt the need to 'be devout' and become a monk. What being or not being devout makes no difference to is the fact that, having been born in a Buddhist country, one is subject to the influence of Buddhist culture whether one practises Buddhism or does not practise it. As Mellor comments, 'in the east one can be a "Buddhist" whether one is devout or not,' the inverted commas indicating that it is Buddhist in the cultural sense that is meant.

Unfortunately, Ajahn Sumedho speaks of a Buddhist society, i.e. a society with a traditionally Buddhist culture, and by implication the members of that society, as 'thinking and living Buddhism', not as being subject, simply, to the influence of traditional Buddhist culture. Though he distinguishes between 'thinking and living Buddhism' and 'being devout', and though 'being devout' means actually practising Buddhism, so that 'thinking and living Buddhism' means *not* practising it, as we have seen, it cannot be denied that the actual phrase 'thinking and living Buddhism' definitely does have a positive connotation suggestive of the practice of Buddhism rather than the contrary. Indeed, I suspect that the majority of people, confronted by the phrases 'thinking and living Buddhism' and 'being devout' (i.e. devoutly Buddhist) would find the former more appealing and more suggestive of the practice of Buddhism than the latter, 'being devout' being associated, in the popular mind, with conventional piety.

Ajahn Sumedho's confusion seems to stem from the fact that he is not sufficiently clear that there is no such thing as a 'born Buddhist', i.e. one who is a Buddhist, without inverted commas, simply by virtue of his having been born in a 'Buddhist' country. He is not sufficiently clear that one is a Buddhist not by birth but only by deeds, just as, in the Buddha's own terminology, one is a brahmin not by birth but only by deeds. 'Born Buddhist' is a contradiction in terms, and failure to realize this means falling into the 'Buddhist' equivalent of orthodox Brahmanism. Being brought up in a Buddhist society, i.e. in a society with a traditional Buddhist culture, is in many ways an inestimable blessing, but one brought up in such a society is himself a Buddhist only if he personally takes advantage of the opportunities for spiritual development that a traditional Buddhist culture provides. Had Ajahn Sumedho been clearer about this he probably would have said, in his interview, something like: 'One has to recognize that Asian teachers have been raised in a society with a traditionally Buddhist culture. Whether they actually practise the Dharma or not does not make any difference to this fact. Nevertheless, that they were raised in such a society affects their whole outlook on themselves and the world.' Had he said this there would be no confusion. But he said what he did say and having said it, and probably half-realized that he had got himself into a muddle, he follows it up with an attack on Western culture, addressing his interviewer directly and saying, 'Whereas you [unlike those brought up in a Buddhist society] come from a culture which is materialistic, and where the values—based on greed and competition, and trust and faith in conceptual learning—have affected our mind.'

It is, of course, true that much of modern Western culture is materialistic, and that many of its values are based on greed and competition, and trust and faith in conceptual learning, but we must not draw too sharp a contrast between materialistic West and idealistic, 'spiritual' East. The culture of a Buddhist country like Thailand, which has between 500,000 and 1,000,000 prostitutes, cannot be described as idealistic without some qualification. In the course of my lengthy sojourn in the Indian subcontinent I came to the conclusion that, although the spiritual traditions of the East are undoubtedly alive in a way that those of the West are not (Christianity having in any case killed off the non-Christian traditions and driven them underground), Asians are, in most cases, no less materialistic—no less greedy and competitive—than Europeans and Americans. The difference is that in the West people are enabled to fulfil their material ambitions by modern technology, whereas in the East they seek, traditionally, to fulfil them by occult or magical means. Since modern technology has increasingly shown itself to be more effective in this respect than rituals and spells, it is rapidly superseding these latter throughout the East—a fact that partly explains why practically the entire Eastern world has either fallen prey to Communism or is succumbing to the influence of capitalism.

3 Having commented on Ajahn Sumedho's more sophisticated understanding of the relationship between religion and culture, and having opined that a faith-decision may be a significant factor in an English context because of the persistence of Protestant orientations, even when it is not formalized into a doctrinal position as in the case of the FWBO, Mellor again represents the Ajahn as speaking of faith-decisions. 'In fact,' he says, 'the English Sangha is critical of the way Buddhist ex-Christians adopt a hostile attitude towards Christianity: one exclusivist faith-decision has been replaced by another one. Ajahn Sumedho rejects such attitudes, asserting that Buddhism is not about faith-decisions but about being able to "find out and know directly".' Whether members of the FWBO are among the Buddhist ex-Christians whom the English Sangha has in mind we need not enquire. Neither need we enquire whether a Buddhist ex-Christian's adoption of a hostile attitude towards Christianity can really be described as the replacement of one exclusivist faith-decision by another, quite apart from the methodological impropriety such an explanation involves. What concerns me is the fact that Mellor, having already represented me as seeing 'becoming a Buddhist' as a faith-decision and as equating this not only with conversion but also with 'a personal decision to "go for refuge"' (*vide supra*, p.140), now cites Ajahn Sumedho as asserting that Buddhism is not about faith-decisions but about being able to 'find out and know directly.' Once again, it is not clear whether Ajahn Sumedho himself actually speaks of 'faith-decisions', but whether he uses the term or not Mellor evidently means to suggest that for me, as one for whom 'a personal decision to "go for refuge"' is a faith-decision, Going for Refuge is *not* about 'being able to "find out and know directly".'

Yet again we are confronted by a misrepresentation, and again that misrepresentation is based on Mellor's failure to understand the FWBO's (fully traditional) teaching on Going for Refuge. Broadly speaking, there are four levels of Going for

Refuge (*vide supra*, p.141), the third of which, real Going for Refuge, takes place when one develops insight and wisdom, thereby entering upon the transcendental Path. Ajahn Sumedho's 'being able to "find out and know directly"' is of the same order as this insight and wisdom, the development of which constitutes real Going for Refuge—assuming that his 'finding out and knowing directly' corresponds to bhāvanāmayā-prajñā or wisdom based on meditation in the sense of the experience of the dhyānas, not to cintāmayā-prajñā or wisdom based on reflection or to śrutamayā-prajñā or wisdom based on learning. Thus Going for Refuge and 'finding out and knowing directly' are not mutually exclusive, as Mellor suggests, and he is able to suggest that they are only because he has categorized Going for Refuge as a faith-decision. Since it is not clear whether Ajahn Sumedho himself actually speaks of 'faith-decisions' and not clear, therefore, whether he categorizes Going for Refuge as a faith-decision, it is also not clear whether, in asserting that Buddhism is about being able to 'find out and know directly', he too is suggesting that Going for Refuge and 'finding out and knowing directly' are mutually exclusive. In any case, the fact that for him Buddhism is about being able to find out and know directly, while for the FWBO (as for the whole Buddhist tradition) real Going for Refuge takes place when one develops insight and wisdom, means that the English Sangha and the FWBO differ less than Mellor thinks.

4 As I have tried to show, Mellor misunderstands and misrepresents the FWBO on a number of issues. But it is not only the FWBO that he misrepresents. He misrepresents the English Sangha. He misrepresents Buddhism. Commenting on Ajahn Sumedho's assertion that Buddhism is 'about being able to find out and know directly', he says, 'This emphasis on knowing directly is indicative of what Sennett terms "a culture ruled by belief in the immediate". In other words, the rejection of one aspect of western culture (the exclusivism of faith-decisions) is balanced by the endorsement of another aspect—the contemporary stress on immediate experience rather than objective belief-systems or knowledges.' Since being able to find out and know directly is of the same order as insight and wisdom, the development of which constitutes real Going for Refuge, Mellor in effect criticizes not only the English Sangha but the FWBO, not to speak of Buddhism itself, and it is therefore not possible for me to ignore the criticism. An 'emphasis on knowing directly', whether that of Ajahn Sumedho or any other Buddhist, is *not* indicative of 'a culture ruled by belief in the immediate' (I overlook the fact that Mellor takes the phrase from Sennett's discussion of the rationality of secular charisma as a way to think about politics) and therefore does *not* amount to an endorsement of the contemporary stress on immediate experience, restricted as such experience is to the physical senses and the lower mind. Like insight and wisdom, direct knowledge is not mundane but transcendental in character, and far from being one-sidedly subjective in the contemporary manner, as Mellor believes, has for 'object' the various 'doors' to the Absolute (*asaṁskṛta-dhātu*) and, ultimately, the Absolute itself. Thus if an emphasis on knowing directly is indicative of anything, it is indicative of continuity with the central tradition of Buddhism, according to which the Dharma is 'to be understood individually, by the wise (*veditabba viññūhi*)' and understood, moreover, by way of what the Buddha of the *Laṅkāvatāra* calls an inner realization (*pratyātma-gocara*). That Mellor should equate Buddhist 'finding out and knowing directly' with the contemporary stress on immediate experience is reductionist in the extreme, and shows how far he is from understanding either the English Sangha or the FWBO or, for the matter of that, Buddhism itself.

5 From Ajahn Sumedho's endorsement of the contemporary stress on immediate experience Mellor passes to what he frankly admits is a contentious subject, albeit one to which the issue of culture and religion in relation to Buddhism is related. The subject is that of 'exoticism' (the inverted commas are his), which for him is 'the extent to which the appeal of Buddhism (or some forms of it) is in any way related to its cultural strangeness.' This is not quite the dictionary definition, but one cannot innocently use the term 'exotic' with reference to Western Buddhism, so Mellor believes, 'merely to refer to something introduced from abroad.' The reason for this, according to him, is that the term has a long history of polemical usage, the perception of Buddhism as being 'exotic' being, in the early development of English Buddhism, both a factor which made it attractive to many Westerners and a polemical tool in the arguments of those who wanted to develop Western forms of it. To what remote period of British Buddhist history the expression 'early development' is meant to refer is not clear, but be that as it may, 'Of this latter tendency [i.e. the tendency to develop Western forms of Buddhism] the FWBO is perhaps the historical fulfilment.' Nor is that all. 'In FWBO discourse the term "exotic" is one of abuse: not only would it resent the use of the term in association with itself, it is actually a favoured term of its own which it uses to attack more (eastern) traditional forms of Buddhism.'

At this point Mellor refers us to *Buddhism for Today*, p.5. On looking up the reference, however, we find that Subhuti does not, in fact, use this term as one of abuse (members of the FWBO prefer, in any case, to avoid using abusive language) but in its primary sense of what is culturally strange. Speaking of the strictly limited appeal and significance of the successive waves of Western interest in Buddhism, he says of these 'waves':

'For the most part, they have attracted the academic and the intellectual, the dilettante, and those who hunger for the exotic; few have been able to accept fully the unique challenge of establishing Buddhism as a living movement at the heart of Western culture.'

If anything is being attacked here, it is *hunger* for the exotic, not the exotic itself, which in any case is never exotic *per se* but only in relation to its (foreign) surroundings or the (foreign) observer. I also wonder what makes Mellor so sure that 'the FWBO' (to him, apparently, a very monolithic body) would 'resent' the use of the term exotic in association with itself. It would depend who used the term. Eastern Buddhists visiting the FWBO have been known to describe it as exotic (i.e. to them culturally strange), and so far as I know this was not resented by anyone. But these are matters of detail. I have shown that Subhuti does *not* use the term exotic as one of abuse. Now let me offer a few comments of my own, both on the term exotic and on the contentious subject of 'exoticism'.

As I have indicated, the primary sense of exotic is culturally strange or 'originating in a foreign country, especially one in the tropics; not native' (*Collins*). British Buddhism, whether as represented by the English Sangha or the FWBO, is exotic in this sense, Buddhism having originated in India 2,500 years ago and from there been introduced into Britain via Ceylon (Sri Lanka), China-Japan, Thailand, etc. British Christianity, too, is exotic in this sense, Christianity having originated in Israel 2,000 years ago and been introduced into Britain via Rome, Germany, Switzerland, etc. Christianity, however, has been established here for so many centuries that it does not *feel* exotic, especially since it has produced such distinctively British forms of Christianity as Anglicanism, Puritanism, Congregationalism, and Methodism; and there is little doubt that the same will be the case with Buddhism after it has been established here for a few hundred years. Meanwhile, British Buddhism is an exotic phenomenon (in the primary sense of the term) *and* is perceived to be such by the general public—a state of affairs that does not particularly trouble me. But the term also has a secondary sense; a sense which Mellor, in his haste to assert that in FWBO discourse the term 'exotic' is one of abuse, fails to notice. Exotic also means 'having a strange or bizarre allure, beauty, or quality' (*Collins*). This kind of allure, beauty, or quality is very much 'in the eye of the beholder', so that unlike the primary sense of the term, which has reference to an objective relation (to the foreign environment or foreign observer), this secondary sense of exotic has reference to a subjective impression or response. Thus whereas the primary sense of the term is *descriptive*, the secondary sense is *evaluative*. There is, of course, nothing wrong in seeing that which is exotic in the primary sense of the term, i.e. culturally strange, or 'originating in a foreign country, especially one in the tropics,' as exotic, also, in the secondary sense of the term, i.e. as 'having a strange or bizarre allure, beauty, or quality'. Why we should see what is merely culturally strange as having this kind of allure, beauty, or quality is a mystery not altogether dispelled by the invocation of that overworked psychological term 'projection'; but there is no doubt that we often do see what is merely culturally strange in this way, especially when we are very young, or when our immediate surroundings are dull and uninspiring. As a boy of thirteen or fourteen, I myself felt the allure and beauty of the South Seas and the Far East as depicted in the colourful pages of Pierre Loti and Lafcadio Hearn.

That some Westerners should find Buddhism exotic in the secondary sense of the term is not surprising. Buddhism is, after all, an exotic religion so far as the West is concerned, i.e. a religion originating in a foreign country. Nor is it surprising that some Westerners should be strongly attracted to this 'exotic Buddhism' of theirs and become involved with it in this or that way. There is nothing actually wrong in seeing Buddhism as exotic in the secondary sense of the term, and nothing actually wrong in being attracted by such 'Buddhism'. What is wrong, or at least mistaken, is thinking (if one thinks about the matter at all) that what one sees is Buddhism itself, in the sense of those ethical and spiritual principles that comprise the Dharma, and that in being attracted to such 'Buddhism' one is aspiring to practise those principles or is even actually practising them already. It is this mistaking of what is, in fact, a Buddhism that is exotic in the (subjective) secondary sense for Buddhism itself that, for me, constitutes exoticism or, in Mellor's words, 'the extent to which the appeal of Buddhism (or some forms of it) is in any way related to its cultural strangeness.'

But while I certainly do regard as wrong, or at least mistaken, the idea that one's (subjectively) exotic Buddhism is Buddhism itself, it is incorrect to speak of me, as Mellor proceeds to do, as offering 'a vision of the English Buddhist as someone who despises the understanding of Buddhism as something exotic'. One does not necessarily despise what one considers mistaken. Having asserted that 'exotic' is a favoured term of the FWBO's own which it uses to attack more (eastern) traditional forms of Buddhism, Mellor continues: 'The rejection of such forms has long been the policy of Sangharakshita. In 1965, while still head of the English Sangha (and thus prior to the creation of the FWBO), Sangharakshita offered a vision of the English Buddhist as someone who despises the understanding of Buddhism as something exotic.' He then quotes from an article on 'Buddhism in England' that I wrote for *The Buddhist*, the journal of the English Sangha Association. By what means he managed to unearth this ancient article from the dusty files of a long defunct Buddhist monthly that never printed more than a few hundred copies is something of a mystery, the more especially since he shows a knowledge of only one of my two dozen published works and seems disinclined to do any research. Strange indeed are the ways of the methodologist! But let me reproduce the quotation. The omissions are Mellor's.

'The English Buddhist has, most often, been attracted to Buddhism on account of the spiritual principles of which it is the embodiment.... He is much less interested in the various national cultures wherein, throughout the traditionally Buddhist cultures of the east, these principles are embedded.... English Buddhism, he hopes, far from remaining a frail transplant carefully sheltered from the chill northern blast in some secluded pseudo-oriental hothouse, will in time develop into a sturdy and vigorous growth.'

I trust Mellor is not suggesting that it is wrong for the English Buddhist to be attracted to Buddhism on account of its spiritual principles, or that he ought to be more, rather than less, interested in the traditionally Buddhist cultures than in these principles. Probably he is not suggesting any such thing, if for no other reason than that for him Buddhism and Buddhist culture are synonymous terms. I also trust he is not suggesting that it is wrong for the English Buddhist to hope that English Buddhism will in time develop into a sturdy and vigorous growth, though in view of Mellor's own religious sympathies one cannot be sure of this. Since my 'vision' of the English Buddhist does not really amount to a rejection of more (eastern) traditional forms of Buddhism (it would be more correct to say that I discriminate among them) I cannot help wondering why Mellor should quote from this article of mine at all, unless it is for the sake of my reference to the 'secluded pseudo-oriental hothouse.' In any case, he goes on to comment, 'It is clear that the FWBO must regard *Amaravati*, the English Sangha's centre, as one such "pseudo-oriental hothouse": its strict adherence to a traditional Buddhist form of practice is a sharp contrast to what Sangharakshita feels is both desirable and necessary to the English Buddhist. As I noted earlier, Sangharakshita draws a clear distinction between the traditionalist approach of the English Sangha and the FWBO's emphasis on only the "essential principles of Buddhism".' I draw, in fact, no such distinction. The distinction I draw, in the interview to which Mellor's note here refers us, is between Tradition with a capital T and tradition with a small T, *not* between a traditionalist and a non-traditionalist approach. To the extent that the FWBO emphasizes 'the essential principles of Buddhism', and thus Tradition with a capital T, its approach could be said to be more truly traditionalist than that of the English Sangha. As for it being clear that the FWBO 'must' regard Amaravati as a pseudo-oriental hothouse, the necessity exists only in Mellor's own mind. I am, however, inclined to think that inasmuch as the English Sangha is culturally more 'eastern' than the FWBO it is more likely to be perceived as being exotic in the secondary sense of the term and more likely, therefore, to be of interest to those who are attracted by 'exotic Buddhism'.

Thus what the English Buddhist of my 'vision' is really saying, when he expresses the hope that English Buddhism will in time develop into a sturdy and vigorous growth, and not remain a frail transplant in some secluded pseudo-oriental hothouse, is not what Mellor supposes. Far from saying that the under-standing of Buddhism as something exotic is to be despised, what he is saying, in effect, is that it is not enough simply to transplant Buddhism to this country. Buddhism must also be-come acclimatized here, and the Buddhism that will become ac-climatized here is the Buddhism that is a matter of universally valid spiritual principles, not the 'exotic Buddhism' that is large-ly a matter of eastern 'Buddhist' culture and which attracts those who, in Subhuti's phrase, hunger for the exotic. The latter may be transplanted but it will not really acclimatize and be-come a sturdy and vigorous growth because it will be depend-ent for its survival on those special (exotic) cultural conditions which the English Buddhist of my vision characterizes as a hothouse, a hothouse which is pseudo-oriental in the sense of being an English imitation of an eastern 'Buddhist' original and secluded in the sense of being remote from English life and thought. If Amaravati is, in fact, a secluded pseudo-oriental hothouse, as Mellor thinks the FWBO must regard it as being, then surely one of the most exotic blooms in that hothouse is the 'white cloth', i.e. the piece of fabric used by monks to receive of-ferings from women without coming into physical contact with them. Being, as it is, a bloom that is unlikely to survive outside its 'Thai' hothouse, it is unlikely that it will ever form part of a sturdy and vigorous English (or British) Buddhism. Future women supporters of the English Sangha *may* embroider 'white cloths' for the monks in much the same way that Victorian spinsters embroidered hassocks and carpet slippers for the local curate, but I rather doubt it. The present women supporters of the Sangha are said to react to the 'white cloth' with either tolerant amusement or feminist outrage.

Having represented the distinction I draw between Tradition with a capital T and tradition with a small T, as a distinction between a traditionalist and a non-traditionalist approach, Mellor is able to repeat some of his old charges against the FWBO. 'Like Christianity,' he says, 'English Buddhism in an eastern, traditional form is given the status of a historically remote precedent to the FWBO. While Subhuti notes the appeal of such forms for "those who hunger for the exotic", he sees the validity of them as lying only in the fact that they "helped to prepare the ground" for the FWBO.' Since I have dealt with these misunderstandings (*vide supra*, pp.86 *et seq* and pp.124 *et seq*) I shall say nothing about them in this place, but will turn straight to Mellor's dig at the FWBO for using Sanskrit names.

6 For Mellor 'exoticism' is the extent to which the appeal of Buddhism (or some forms of it) is in any way related to its cultural strangeness. Directly after referring to the fact that Subhuti notes the appeal of the eastern, traditional forms of Buddhism for 'those who hunger for the exotic' he is therefore able to say: 'Nevertheless, if by "exotic" we refer to a cultural foreignness then it is ironic that the FWBO is hardly free of an overt exoticism either. Sangharakshita uses the full title of Ven. Maha Sthavira Sangharakshita rather than "Dennis Lingwood", FWBO communities have names such as "Padmaloka", and members use Sanskrit names prefaced by "Dharmachari" or "Dharmacharini" (practitioners of the *Dharma*), though there is no traditional precedent for the use of Sanskrit names in this way.' It is not ironic at all. It is not ironic because I distinguish between that which is exotic in the primary sense of the term, i.e. which simply originates in a foreign country, and that which is exotic in the secondary sense, i.e. which in addition to originating in a foreign country has a strange or bizarre allure, beauty, or quality (*vide supra*, p.156 *et seq*). Thus the FWBO's use of foreign (Indian) names does not mean that it is 'hardly free of an overt exoticism' but only that it is exotic inasmuch as Buddhism has its origin in a foreign country. We shall return to the subject of exotic nomenclature later. Meanwhile, let me make two points. Firstly, I stopped using the title 'Maha Sthavira' some years ago, as Mellor would have realized if he had looked at the title page of my more recent publications. I stopped using it mainly because an increasing number of Buddhist (and Hindu) teachers were awarding themselves such titles as 'His Holiness' and 'His Eminence' and I wanted to dissociate myself from a trend which, to me, smacked more of worldly ambition than of spiritual achievement. Friends and disciples of long standing, especially those in India, still address me as 'Maha Sthavira', whether from force of habit or out of respect. In recent years some of my Western disciples have taken to addressing me as 'Urgyen Sangharakshita', Urgyen being the name I was given by my teacher Kachu Rimpoche in 1962 on the occasion of my receiving the Padmasambhava abhiṣekha or 'Tantric initiation'. Secondly, it is not clear what Mellor means when he claims that there is no traditional precedent for using Sanskrit names 'in this way', i.e. in the way they are used in the FWBO. In Indian Buddhism there are innumerable traditional precedents for the use of Sanskrit names, both for dwelling places and for persons, and innumerable precedents for the use of the literal translations of Sanskrit names in Chinese, Japanese, and Tibetan Buddhism. What Mellor means is therefore a mystery.

Mystery or no mystery, however, the question of the FWBO's use of Sanskrit names continues to bother him. Referring to my interview with him, he says, 'Questioned about this adoption of Sanskrit names Sangharakshita rejected any charge of inconsistency, arguing that the maintenance of Christian names was inappropriate, that taking a new name had an important psychological effect, and that Sanskrit would provide a unifying characteristic of the FWBO across different cultures "in the way that Latin used to in the Catholic Church".' Since the subject of exotic nomenclature is being dealt with later, I shall take up first the question of Sanskrit as providing a unifying characteristic of the FWBO in the way that Latin used to in the Catholic Church, this being what Mellor himself takes up first. 'This latter comparison hardly seems justified,' he sneers. 'The FWBO's development outside Britain seems less successful than that of the English Sangha which now has branches in the USA, Australia, New Zealand and Switzerland.' Once again, Mellor has got his facts wrong. So very wrong, indeed, that his assertion would be truer if names were transposed and it read: 'The English Sangha's development outside Britain seems less successful than that of the FWBO which now has branches [i.e. autonomous centres run by teams of Order members] in the USA, Australia, New Zealand, India, Holland, Finland, Sweden, Germany, and Spain.' Since at least nine languages are involved here (India supplying three), the use of Sanskrit (and Pali) for liturgical and other purposes does indeed provide a unifying characteristic for the FWBO across different cultures, as I can testify from repeated personal experience. Mellor's sneer about my comparison with the use of Latin by the Catholic Church being unjustified is therefore itself unjustified. But there is another sneer to come.

'The FWBO makes a great deal of its connection with Ambedkar's movement of "ex-untouchables" in India, but there is little objective evidence for FWBO strength in a movement Trevor Ling has called only "neo-Buddhist". In fact, although Ling refers to Sangharakshita's writings on Ambedkar, and to a series of lectures he gave at one point, not once in a fairly detailed study of Ambedkar's movement does he mention the FWBO.' This is perfectly true. Trevor Ling does not once mention the FWBO in his *Buddhist Revival in India*. But had Mellor examined the book more carefully he would have noticed that it was published in 1980, after key chapters had appeared in academic journals and elsewhere as early as 1973. The FWBO, on the other hand, was not formally inaugurated in India (as the TBMSG or Trailokya Bauddha Mahasangha Sahayak Gana) until 1979, when the first Indian Order members were ordained. Thus Mellor's information is at least twelve years out of date. If he is really interested in obtaining 'objective evidence' for the strength of the FWBO in Ambedkar's movement, rather than in sneering at its supposed lack of strength there, then I suggest he does a little research among the back issues of *Golden Drum* and the Karuna Trust *Newsletter*, or better still, does a little field work and visits at least some of the FWBO's nine Dharma Centres which, between them, conduct activities in more than one hundred places in India. It is also perfectly true that the FWBO 'makes a great deal of its connection with Ambedkar's movement of "ex-untouchables",' though not in the kind of way Mellor implies. We make much of it for a number of reasons, not least because the fact that our ex-Untouchable brothers and sisters tend to approach Buddhism from a social angle, whereas we in the West tend to approach it more psychologically, helps us to correct our one-sidedness and thus to create a more balanced attitude on the part of the FWBO as a whole.

From the FWBO's connection with Ambedkar's movement Mellor returns to the question of exotic nomenclature, and we must return with him. 'Sangharakshita's first reason for using Sanskrit names, that they did not want to use Christian ones,' he proceeds, 'is perhaps more significant. One of the major distinguishing features of the FWBO is its outright hostility to Christianity. Despite the insignificance the FWBO attaches to culture generally, western names and (Christian) religion *do* coincide in a way which is uncomfortable for the FWBO: because of this, Sanskrit names *are* appealing because they are exotic; that is, they are attractive because they are culturally alien.' Whether hostility to Christianity, outright or otherwise, is a 'major' distinguishing feature of the FWBO (part of its essence, as it were?), is debatable; but there is no doubt that in the last sentence quoted the number of misrepresentations is high even by Mellorian standards. I shall therefore have to deal with each of them separately. They relate to (a) the 'insignificance' the FWBO attaches to culture, (b) the 'uncomfortable' way in which, for the FWBO, Western names and (Christian) religion coincide, and (c) the 'exotic' appeal of Sanskrit names.

(a) Mellor does not define culture, of course, but if we take the word in its generally accepted sense, especially as relating to literature, the fine arts, drama, and music, then it is clear that he has not read, or not heeded, either Chapter 10 of Subhuti's *Buddhism for Today*, entitled 'Beauty is Truth', or my own early essay 'The Religion of Art'. Having pointed out that 'Buddhist cultures flowered many times throughout the East,' Subhuti proceeds, a few pages later, to emphasize the importance of culture in a way that illustrates how little 'insignificance' the FWBO attaches to it.

'The appreciation of the arts and their value for the developing individual is strongly encouraged within the FWBO. Many Centres organise poetry readings, concerts, and other cultural activities, and lectures and study groups are often held on artists and their works. Many people find that, for the first time, they acquire an appreciation of such things as they deepen their experience of meditation. They are able to overcome the associations which art has for them of effete foppishness and boredom—the one the result of the prevailing directionlessness of much modern art, the other of the spiritless force-feeding of school. Many Order members and Friends find, now, a deep source of inspiration in some works of both Western and Eastern culture.'[52]

The only way we can make sense of Mellor's belief that the FWBO attaches 'insignificancc' to culture generally is by assuming that for him culture is an essentially group phenomenon and that he sees the FWBO, therefore, as regarding culture as being insignificant in comparison with the individual. But even so the FWBO cannot be described as attaching 'insignificance' to culture generally, especially inasmuch as the distinctively Western Buddhist culture of its envisagement will be the product, in part, of interaction between Western Buddhists and elements of both Eastern (Buddhist) and Western culture (*vide supra*, p.145). Once again a little field work on Mellor's part would not be out of place, particularly if this was to take him to FWBO centres in both East and West.

(b) Western forenames and (Christian) religion obviously coincide, though with less inevitability now than they did in more God-fearing times. What Mellor means by saying that they coincide 'in a way that is uncomfortable for the FWBO' is less obvious. He seems to think he has scored a point, as though the fact of names and (Christian) religion coinciding in a way that is 'uncomfortable for the FWBO' somehow constitutes an argument against it or exposes a weakness in its understanding of the relationship between religion and culture. He also seems to regard the FWBO as a monolithic abstraction that is somehow susceptible to feelings of collective discomfort. The reality is far otherwise. The FWBO consists of individuals. Some of those individuals were brought up as Christians, and not a few who were brought up as Christians have been psychologically damaged by the experience, in some cases to such an extent that during the early years of their involvement with the FWBO they have to spend much of their time trying to repair the damage. For such ex-Christians, names and (Christian) religion coincide in a way that is not just uncomfortable but positively painful. One unfortunate woman, now an Order member, was christened Anne Maria Theresa Bernadette, and Mellor will perhaps understand the relief she felt when, on the occasion of her ordination, she was at last able to relinquish this blatantly Christian and Roman Catholic appellation, with all the unpleasant associations it had come to have for her, and receive in its place a name more in accordance with her spiritual aspirations.

(c) Or perhaps he will not understand. We must not forget that Mellor is not only emphatic that 'Despite the insignificance the FWBO attaches to culture generally, western names and (Christian) religion *do* coincide in a way that is uncomfortable for the FWBO.' He is also emphatic that 'because of this, Sanskrit names *are* appealing because they are exotic; that is, they are attractive because they are culturally alien.' This is certainly not the case, nor does it even follow that it is the case from Mellor's own (mistaken) premise. Whether as names of dwelling places or names of persons, Sanskrit names, i.e. Sanskrit (and Pali) *Buddhist* names, do *not* appeal to members of the FWBO because they are exotic; they do *not* find them attractive because they are naturally alien. Sanskrit names appeal to members of the FWBO because they embody Buddhist principles or Buddhist precepts, or because they are the names of historical or mythical Buddhist personages, so that as often as we use those names we are reminded of those principles, precepts, or personages and of our own connection with them. Order members are always very much aware of the meaning of their 'Order names', the significance of which is explained to them at the time of their ordination and subsequently to the Movement at large.

The last paragraph of this section of Mellor's article is devoted to the role exoticism plays in the appeal or character of the English Sangha. Since Thai monasticism judges itself against a 'pristine model' that, in the case of the English Sangha, has been identified with Ajahn Chah's forest monasteries in Thailand, these monasteries, and indeed traditional Buddhism and traditionally Buddhist cultures, become immune from criticism. 'When Ajahn Sumedho draws a distinction between eastern and western culture,' Mellor reminds us, 'it is the *western* which is criticized. Unlike the FWBO which only rejects those elements in western culture which it associates with hostility to the development of the individual, the English Sangha rejects western culture on a greater scale: since western culture is associated with "greed and competition", materialism, self-absorption and decadence, traditional Buddhist cultures bask in the reflected glow of the pristine Thai model. Thus,' he concludes, 'the foreignness of traditional Buddhist cultures does have an exotic appeal for Buddhists associated with the English Sangha.' This is very much in accordance with my own comment (*vide supra*, p.160) that inasmuch as the English Sangha is culturally more 'eastern' than the FWBO it is more likely to be perceived as exotic in the secondary sense of the term and more likely, therefore, to be of interest to those who are attracted by 'exotic Buddhism'.

MELLOR APPEARS to draw a distinction between cultural translation and cultural transferral, though it is only at the very end of the present section of his article, the fifth and last, that we are given an inkling of the nature of this distinction. Cultural transferral would seem to refer to Buddhism's bodily removal, so to speak, from Thailand or Tibet to Britain, much as the Virgin Mary's house was carried by angels lock stock and barrel from Nazareth to Loreto in central Italy. Cultural translation, on the other hand, refers to the fact that in 'entering western culture' (whatever that may mean) Buddhism 'has become the focus for an interaction between eastern and western religious forms, creating discourses which are Buddhist but which have at the same time many of the features of Protestant Christian discourse.' Thus 'translation' does not mean quite what we may have thought it meant. It does not mean the expression of an identical meaning in a different medium, as when a sentence is rendered from one language into another, nor does it mean the expression of one mode or degree of knowledge in terms of another mode or degree of knowledge, as it does in my paper 'St Jerome Revisited'—St Jerome being the Translator *par excellence* of Western (i.e. Latin Christian) tradition. For Mellor there does not exist a something that is translated as distinct from a something into which it is translated.

This is evident from the way his brief discussion of cultural translation opens. Any simple interpretation of the cultural translation of Buddhism into England is problematic, he declares. It is problematic because 'for the purposes of academic analysis it is difficult to isolate the "Buddhism" which is being "translated".' What Mellor means by *academic* analysis, and why it should be necessary to subject Buddhism to it, I do not know, though I cannot help feeling it has something to do with 'murdering to dissect'. Probably he means analysing Buddhism in terms of sociological and methodological categories that are foreign to it. But be that as it may, the reason it is difficult to isolate the 'Buddhism' which is being 'translated' is that 'if we separate a Buddhist form from all its cultural "expressions" and then consider how it is modified as it moves from one culture to another, then we are accepting the philosophical position of the FWBO as normative for academic analysis. We would also be basing our analysis on a signifier of perspectives critical to liberal Protestantism. If my discussion had proceeded on this basis then many of the major philosophical problems which have been considered would not only have been avoided, but may not even have been apparent.'

This is a very curious argument indeed. It is rather like saying that we cannot base our astronomy on the Copernican system because if we did so base it many of the problems associated with the Ptolemaic theory of epicycles would not only be avoided, but may not even be apparent. Mellor is also guilty of arguing *ad hominem*. We cannot separate a Buddhist form from its cultural 'expressions' and then consider how it is modified as it moves from one country to another, because then we should be accepting the philosophical position of the FWBO. Why we should not accept the philosophical position of the FWBO, and why that position should not be normative for academic analysis, is not explained. Neither is there any explanation why we should not base our analysis on a signifier of perspectives critical to liberal Protestantism, the falsity of such perspectives apparently being regarded as self-evident. There is also the assumption that the philosophical position of the FWBO and the perspectives critical to liberal Protestantism are somehow bound up with each other; but as I have shown in my critique of the second section of Mellor's article, 'Protestantism and Buddhism', the FWBO cannot really be regarded as demonstrating continuities with these perspectives.

Despite his rejection of what he styles the FWBO's philosophical position, i.e. the position that a Buddhist form is separable from its cultural expressions, Mellor is aware that 'if we ... locate religion firmly within culture we are faced with another set of problems.' These problems are of a practical nature. 'In the final analysis,' he is forced to admit, 'it is difficult to see how such a model could cope with religious change at all, since all religion would be culture-bound, and therefore static. Even if a certain amount of dynamism was allowed into the model— religion is culture-bound but cultures can interact—it still could not deal with all the variables.' This is very true, and it is one of the reasons for my rejection of this particular model. Even if the FWBO's own model was found to be inadequate, there would still be a need for a model that could cope with religious change, which Mellor appears to think inevitable. The 'static' model of which Mellor speaks is, of course, the model with which the English Sangha seeks to align itself, and he therefore continues: 'For example, the English Sangha legitimates its adoption of eastern traditions and rituals on the grounds that religion cannot be so easily separated from culture: the English Sangha adopts the entire practice of Thai monasticism (as far as it can) because it is not confident about what can be discarded and what cannot.' As we have seen, it is not sure whether or not the 'white cloth' can be discarded. 'It does not seek to separate religion from culture. However, despite this orientation towards tradition the English Sangha *does* separate religion from culture as is shown by its very existence: rejecting its own (English) cultural models, it adopts a foreign (Thai) one.'

The observation is just. The English Sangha adopts Buddhism *and* Thai culture because it regards religion and culture as inseparable. Yet in order to do this it has to reject its own (English) culture (the fact that Ajahn Sumedho is an American does not really affect the argument), which means it regards culture as separable. Thus according to Mellor the English Sangha's position is hopelessly self-contradictory. The Sangha could, of course, rejoin (I do not know if it actually would) that not only does it regard Buddhism and Thai culture as inseparable; it also regards Christianity and Western culture as inseparable, and that besides adopting Buddhism *and* Thai culture it rejects Western culture *and* Christianity. But this would mean English (and American) Buddhists having to pretend to be Thai Buddhists, in which case they would either have to go and live permanently in Thailand (as some have done) or create a Little Thailand in Britain (as others are trying to do). In neither case would there be a Western Buddhism, but at best only a 'cultural transferral' of Thai Buddhism to this country.

1 Now that he has come practically to the end of his article, Mellor would seem to want to strike a balance. His study, he tells us, 'has considered the relationship between religion and culture to be neither one of complete separation nor exclusive identity. Instead, this relationship has been understood as one of mutual definition and influence, though not without different sets of restrictions, on either side, according to context.' My own impression, throughout Mellor's article, has been that he considers religion and culture to be more or less identical and that his personal sympathies are, therefore, with the traditionalist English Sangha rather than the (supposedly) anti-traditionalist FWBO. But it could be that he has, all the time, been acting devil's advocate and criticizing the FWBO more strongly than he really thought was justified. In any case, he goes on to give what may be considered the rationale of his article. 'Because various discourses centred around Buddhism have been the object of study, rather than the translation of a pre-determined intellectual formation the analyst labels "Buddhism" (whether it is the doctrinal Buddhism of philosophy or the "practical" Buddhism of anthropology), a range of relationships between English Buddhism and both western and eastern culture has been considered which might otherwise have been left unexplored.' The fallaciousness of such a position has already been exposed. Here I might only add that Mellor rejects the idea of studying 'the translation of a pre-determined intellectual formation the analyst labels "Buddhism"' only to embrace that of studying a no less pre-determined intellectual formation he labels 'English Buddhism' or 'English Buddhist group'. If Buddhism cannot be defined, because it has no 'essence', then 'Buddhist' cannot be defined either. Even discourses 'centred around Buddhism' cannot be studied or discussed, since they are the discourses of *Buddhists*, i.e. those who accept the pre-determined intellectual formation 'Buddhism', whether as members of the English Sangha or members of the FWBO. Thus unless we accept a 'Buddhism' there can be no Buddhists and, therefore, no Buddhist discourses centred around Buddhism. As I commented in connection with the idea that there is an 'essence of Buddhism', discourse implies definition, and definition implies essence (*vide supra*, p.47).

'Some of the major differences between the FWBO and the English Sangha are due not only to their different attitudes to eastern religious practices, but also to certain western discourses/practices, especially modernism which the FWBO embraces and the English Sangha despises.' This is hardly correct. Besides showing that there are fewer differences between the FWBO and the English Sangha than Mellor thinks, I have made it clear, in my comments on the third section of his article, entitled 'Modernism and Buddhism', that the FWBO is far from embracing modernism. 'In terms of such continuities, and disruptions, the whole issue of the influence of liberal Protestant perspectives cannot be addressed if the analysis is firmly anchored to the idea of an essential Buddhism which is being translated.' No doubt it cannot, from Mellor's point of view. But neither can it be addressed if we reject the idea of essence and, therewith, both definition and the possibility of discourse, including discourse on the influence of liberal Protestant perspectives.

2 Mellor would also seem to want to show his impartiality, as between the FWBO and the English Sangha. At any rate, he concludes his study with a parting shot at English Buddhism in general, for which he appears to feel a distaste amounting to positive dislike. But though Mellor fires the shot, this time it is Edward Conze who is (posthumously) conscripted into loading the gun. 'Finally,' he says, 'I suggest that this discussion has shown that "Buddhism" in England is a deeply problematic category.' The inverted commas are no doubt meant to emphasize just how deeply problematic that category is. 'It [i.e. "Buddhism" in England] is the focus for a number of different, sometimes competing, religious and cultural forces. While Buddhism is a religion of eastern origin, in England it has become part of a liberal Protestant trend, even though it still might manifest itself in an ostentatiously Asian mode.' Presumably it is *not* the FWBO that is under attack in the last part of this sentence, our 'mode' not being Asian in the West and not 'ostentatiously' Asian even in India. However, Mellor continues: 'One of the leading scholars of Buddhism this century, Edward Conze, has noted the Protestant character of Buddhism in the west: "Buddhist societies have sprung up for nearly eighty years, chiefly in Protestant countries. There they form one of the smaller Nonconformist sects".' Dear old Edward Conze (whom I knew personally) was certainly one of the leading scholars of Buddhism this century, but his field of expertise was the Prajñāpāramitā or 'Perfection of Wisdom' literature, not the sociology of Western Buddhism; moreover, he delighted in being deliberately provocative at the expense of the then British Buddhist establishment. His comment on the 'Protestant character of Buddhism in the west' cannot be regarded as being anything but a *jeu d'esprit*, the more especially since the work from which Mellor quotes was originally published (in Italian) in 1958. Mellor also overlooks the fact that Conze is speaking of Buddhist *societies*, the limitations of which are spelled out in Subhuti's *Buddhism for Today*, p.25.

Conze's use of the term 'Nonconformist' is *not* overlooked, however. In fact Mellor seizes upon it. 'This reference to Non-conformism is pertinent,' he assures us. It is pertinent because 'there is an element of cultural rebellion in western people adopting Buddhism as a religion.' If there is an element of cultural rebellion in western people adopting Buddhism as a religion, there is an even greater element of *religious* rebellion— but Mellor does not mention this, presumably because he tends to think of religion and culture as being more or less identical. He continues: 'Buddhist groups emphasize the significance of this rebellion, suggesting that western culture generally is in a state of decay and needs a radical reorientation such as Buddhism can provide.' In the case of the FWBO, at least, this emphasis is selective: some areas of western culture are *not* in a state of decay and need a less radical reorientation than others. As Mellor himself recognizes, the FWBO does not reject all elements in Western culture, but only those which it associates with hostility to the development of the individual (*vide supra*, p.167). In fact it is not Western culture that is in a state of decay so much as Western religion. By this I do not mean that Christianity is in state of decay (though it may be, on its own terms), but rather that traditional Christianity is itself a state of decay. So much is this the case that for the last few hundred years it is secular literature, secular art, secular music, and secular philosophy that have been the principal bearers of spiritual values in the West, not religion, even though the old Christian forms and symbols have continued to be made use of to some extent. As Middleton Murry puts it in 'Romantics and Tradition', written in reply to T.S. Eliot, 'With the Renaissance the stream of religious tradition began to flow outside the Church. Science took upon itself the fulfilment of the outward exploration, literature the fulfilment of the inward exploration of life.'[53] Or as the same writer says, even more pithily, in 'The "Classical" Revival', 'England rejected Catholicism four centuries ago. And with the rejection of Catholicism English literature began.'[54] Literature being, for

Murry, the principal bearer of spiritual values, at least in England.

Not only is there an element of cultural rebellion in western people adopting Buddhism as a religion, with Buddhist groups emphasizing the significance of this rebellion, thus suggesting that Western culture generally is in a state of decay and in need of a radical reorientation such as Buddhism can provide. According to Mellor, Ling goes so far as to argue that Western Buddhist groups may signify an important cultural development. This is a possibility Mellor himself does not contemplate with equanimity, and he moves to contain any such development within his own perspectives. 'However, as Conze indicates,' he assures us, 'this desire for an "alternative" type of society, takes place broadly within the established religious context of western culture. Buddhist groups in England are a "significant new cultural development" not because they divert western culture into new religious channels, but because they explore the existing religious channels in new ways. Their significance rests in their ability to create new religious forms within liberal Protestant culture.' In the case of the FWBO, at least, this is not true. However much or however little it may 'divert' Western culture into new religious channels, it certainly does not explore existing religious channels in new ways. Nontheism is not a new way of exploring theism; meditation is not a new way of exploring prayer. As for the FWBO's significance resting on its ability to create new religious forms within liberal Protestant culture, this present 'protest and affirmation' of mine has, I trust, shown the ludicrousness of any such assertion. Hence while agreeing with Mellor that 'Buddhism has not been "transferred" [bodily] into this culture, but has been "translated",' I cannot agree with him that such translation consists in the fact that 'in entering western culture it has become the focus for an interaction between eastern and western religious forms, creating discourses which are Buddhist but which have at the same time many of the features of Protestant Christian

discourse.' So far as the FWBO is concerned, the cultural translation of Buddhism consists in the fact that on finding itself in a
Western environment it has become the focus for an interaction
between the timeless truths of the Dharma and the language of
the secular Western culture through which it seeks to express
those truths. Western Buddhism is/will be the creation of that
interaction.

DEAR DR ZAEHNER, having just read your *Evolution in Religion*, I am writing to say how greatly it has interested me and how much I find myself, as a Buddhist, in general agreement with the spirit of your approach. Interpretations of religion in 'evolutionary' terms nowadays seem to be rather 'in the air' and a comparative study such as yours, which compares two such prominent representatives of the evolutionary approach as the Hindu Aurobindo and the Catholic Teilhard, is undoubtedly to be welcomed. I would like, however, to make a few comments on your references to Buddhism, as well as to suggest that Buddhism, too, can be approached from the point of view of evolution.

In Chapter 1, 'Religion and Religions', you point out that Teilhard and Aurobindo at least agree in thinking that Vedānta, Marxism, and Christianity are the only possible alternatives before mankind. You yourself, however, draw attention to the 'striking omission' of Islām, rightly questioning whether it can be written off quite so easily even from the 'integral' and 'convergent' point of view. For you, therefore, there are apparently four alternatives before mankind: Vedānta, Marxism, Christianity, and Islām. Having done justice to Islām, you recollect that besides the four 'alternatives' there are usually reckoned to be five other 'great' religions of the world. Zoroastrianism, Confucianism, and Taoism are rightly dismissed as virtually extinct, while Judaism, like Hinduism, remains the religion of a nation. Of its very nature it cannot become a world religion. As you say, there remains only Buddhism. Why, then, do neither Teilhard nor Aurobindo mention it? While agreeing with your explanation for their comparative silence, I wish to challenge the assumption upon which that silence is based—an assumption which you seem to share.

Briefly, the assumption seems to be that Buddhism can be reduced to its Theravāda form, or to Zen, or to a combination of the two. Surely this is like assuming that Christianity can be reduced to the Greek Orthodox Church, or to Methodism, or to a combination of both of these. In either case what may fairly be regarded as the central tradition of the religion concerned has been entirely omitted from consideration. The central tradition of Buddhism, broadly speaking, is that of the Mahāyāna, regarded as subsuming the Sarvāstivāda tradition, as consisting 'philosophically' of the Yogācāra-Mādhyamīka Schools, and as finding practical spiritual expression in terms of the Bodhisattva Ideal. This central tradition of Buddhism is/was the one dominant principally in China, Japan, Tibet, Korea, Mongolia, and Vietnam. Since Vedānta is really inseparable from Hinduism, for me the alternatives before mankind are: Marxism, Buddhism, Christianity, and Islām. Indeed, I would argue that Buddhism occupies, in a sense, a middle position between Marxism on the one hand and Christianity and Islām on the other. Like Marxism Buddhism is non-theistic, and like Christianity and Islām it is a spiritual teaching as distinct from a form of materialism. It is this union of the non-theistic and the spiritual which, I believe, constitutes one of the great strengths of Buddhism, especially at the present time, giving it, for opposite reasons, a decided advantage over both the atheist-materialist and the theistic-spiritual alternatives.

Incidentally, Aurobindo seems to have been afflicted with as strange a blindness with regard to Buddhism as Teilhard with regard to Eastern mysticism in general. Some twenty years ago, when I first read *The Life Divine*, I was astonished to find him again and again referring to the Buddhist Nirvāṇa as a purely negative state. In so widely read a man as Sri Aurobindo this amounted to wilful ignorance: even in the Theravāda Nirvāṇa is not regarded as a state of pure negation of mundane existence.

Besides occupying a middle position between the atheist-materialist and the theistic-spiritual alternatives, Buddhism is more open to an approach in terms of evolution than either Christianity or Hinduism. Teilhard's evolutionary interpretation of Catholicism strikes me, indeed, as something of a *tour de force*, and you are no doubt right in transferring to him the appellation of poet with which you were honoured in Delhi. In the case of Aurobindo, though his intentions are noble, even sublime, I do not think that much is likely to emerge from the cloud of words in which he has involved a few vague ideas. (Prompted by your quotations, I have just re-read *Thoughts and Aphorisms*, and am surprised how flat and essentially commonplace these sayings of his are. One has only to think of Blake's *Proverbs of Hell* to appreciate this.) Both Teilhard's and Aurobindo's spiritual evolutionism would seem, in fact, to go against the grain of their respective religions, and I am inclined to doubt if Christianity or Hinduism will be much affected by the thought of either of them. In the case of Buddhism, however, an approach from the point of view of evolution would seem to be very much in accordance with the genius of the tradition itself. Four considerations could be cited, among others, in support of this contention. You are, I am sure, familiar with them, though you may never have seen them quite in this light.

1. In one form or another, the concept of the Path has always been central to Buddhism. The Path consists of steps or stages. These steps or stages represent, essentially, states of consciousness, or of being, which are progressive, leading the individual from ignorance to Enlightenment, from the condition of *pṛthagjana* to that of Arhant or Buddha. One could therefore say that the conception of spiritual development, or spiritual *evolution* (what I call the Higher Evolution of Man) is central to Buddhism.

2. It is well known that there grew up round the Buddha a Sangha which continued after his death and still exists today. Ideally this Sangha is a purely spiritual sodality, an 'Assembly

of the Elect,' whether monk or lay, who have attained the higher spiritual stages of the Path, and who, being incapable of regression, are assured of Nirvāṇa. This Sangha is the nucleus of an ideal community and it stands in the same relation to society at large as the individual *ārya* stands to the individual *pṛthagjana*. Thus spiritual evolution is clearly seen not only as individual but as collective.

3. As already stated, the central tradition of Buddhism, the Mahāyāna, finds practical expression in terms of the Bodhisattva Ideal. This represents much more than a personal ideal for ethical and spiritual behaviour. The figure of the Bodhisattva is the concrete embodiment of the principle of spiritual evolution, both individual and cosmic. The Bodhisattva Ideal being ubiquitous in the Mahāyāna, this principle is by implication ubiquitous too.

4. The Buddhist Scriptures, especially those of the Mahāyāna, quite clearly envisage a universe (in the fullest sense of the term) in which, under the guidance of Buddhas and Bodhisattvas innumerable, all sentient beings are ultimately destined to Enlightenment, even the Devadattas of the world not being excluded. In this sense one may therefore speak of Buddhism as the religion of evolution, of spiritual evolution, on a cosmic scale. Indeed, in texts such as the *Saddharma-puṇḍarīka* this is exactly how the Mahāyāna sees itself. No *tour de force* of interpretation is necessary.

Though I have been preoccupied with Buddhism for thirty years, the fact that it was possible to approach Buddhism from the point of view of evolution,—that Buddhism, more than any other religion, indeed was the leading historical embodiment of the principle of spiritual evolution,—was far from being immediately apparent to me. For many years I was much more concerned with the practical problem of striving actually to follow the Path in the traditional manner than with any attempt to reinterpret it in contemporary terms. The realization that *Buddhism was the Higher Evolution* dawned on me only gradually, and my approach to it was oblique. Three main stages can perhaps be distinguished.

1. According to tradition, the Buddha's Enlightenment consisted in an insight into the truth of universal conditionality. This insight found conceptual expression in the fundamental teaching of the chain of 'Dependent Origination' (*pratītya-samutpāda*). With the help of Dr Beni Madhab Barua and Mrs C.A.F. Rhys Davids I discovered that this chain was not limited to an explanation of the process of repeated existence in the world, particularly of the phenomenon of human suffering, as was generally supposed, but also included the Path leading from the world to Nirvāṇa. In its entirety it in fact consisted not of one series of twelve links but of two, the first series being cyclical in character, the second progressive. This meant, in effect, that the Path to Enlightenment could not be reduced to the gradual cessation of the mundane but possessed a definite nature of its own. In other words, Buddhism was not just negative asceticism. Nirvāṇa was not annihilation. All this I have explained in full detail in *A Survey of Buddhism* (1957) Chapter One, XIV.

2. Contemplating the twelve links that made up the missing half of the chain of Dependent Origination, the true nature of the Path became clear to me. It was not a thing of artificial steps and stages. Neither was it a succession of observances. Essentially, it consisted of a sequence of psychological and spiritual experiences. These experiences were not only progressive but cumulative. Between them they constituted a process of continuous growth and development by which the individual advanced from lower to higher states of being and consciousness. This process could well be termed not only a development but even an evolution. The twelve positive *nidānas*, as I term them, are explained at length in Part II, 13, 'The Stages of the Path', of my book *The Three Jewels* (1967).

3. So far my realization that Buddhism was the Path of the Higher Evolution had remained within a strictly traditional

framework. In 1964, however, having spent twenty years in the East, I returned to England, and soon felt the need, purely as a 'skilful means' (*upāya-kausalya*) of a principle sufficiently familiar to the modern mind not to require much explanation and capable, at the same time, of being generalized in such a way as to provide a medium for the exposition of Buddhism. One day, while preparing a lecture, it flashed on me that the concept of Evolution was such a principle. At once everything fell into place. Science revealed how far man had come. This was the Lower Evolution. Buddhism, as the Path, showed how far he still had to go. This was the Higher Evolution. Though not strictly continuous the two phases between them constituted the halves of a single process. Science and religion, the Lower and the Higher Evolution, were comprehended in one gigantic sweep. In the course of the last few years I have developed these ideas in detail, thus working out an approach to Buddhism in terms of Evolution. So far I have not written any book on the subject, though I have dealt with it in several courses of lectures, the most important such course being the eight lectures on 'The Higher Evolution of Man' (Autumn 1969).

To what extent these words will be able to convey to you the nature of my evolutionary vision of Buddhism I do not know. They may well be too obscure to convey anything at all. Nevertheless, I venture to hope that they will at least serve to indicate the existence of an attempt to approach Buddhism, too, from the point of view of evolution, and that as such,—as well as evidence of the interest your book has excited,—you will welcome them.

Yours sincerely,
Sangharakshita
Muswell Hill, London N.10.
9th August 1971

P.S. In case you would like to follow up the references I have given, I am asking the publishers to send you a copy of *A Survey of Buddhism* and of *The Three Jewels*.

1 Dharmachari Kulananda, 'Protestant Buddhism', *Religion* Vol.22, January 1992, pp.101–103
2 Sangharakshita, *My Relation to the Order*, Windhorse, Glasgow 1990, p.35
3 Thomas McEvilley, 'Plotinus and Vijñānavāda Buddhism', in *Philosophy East and West 30*, no.2, University Press of Hawaii, April 1980, pp.181–194; Richard T. Wallis, 'Phraseology and Imagery in Plotinus and Indian Thought', in R. Baine Harris (ed.), *Neoplatonism and Indian Thought*, State University of New York Press, Albany 1990, pp.101–120
4 Sangharakshita, *New Currents in Western Buddhism: The Inner Meaning of the Friends of the Western Buddhist Order*, Windhorse, Glasgow 1990, pp.18–9
5 Timothy Ward, *What the Buddha Never Taught*, Element, 1990
6 R. Sennett, *The Fall of Public Man*, Cambridge University Press, 1974, p.4
7 E. Shils, *Tradition*, Faber and Faber, London 1981, p.11
8 Ibid, p.4
9 Ibid, p.43
10 L. Dumont, 'A modified view of our origins: The Christian beginnings of modern individualism', in M. Carrithers, S. Collins, and S. Luke (eds.), *The Category of the Person*, Cambridge University Press, 1986, pp.117–8
11 L. Dumont, *Homo Hierarchicus*, Paladin, London 1962, p.39
12 Malcolm Woodfield (ed.), *Defending Romanticism: Selected Criticism of John Middleton Murry*, Bristol Press, 1991 (paperback edition), p.131
13 F.L. Woodward (trans.), *The Book of the Kindred Sayings (Saṁyutta-Nikāya)*, Part III, Kegan Paul Trench Trubner Ltd, London, pp.24–25. See also Edward J. Thomas, *The History of Buddhist Thought*, London 1933, p.100

14 L. Dumont, op. cit., p.95
15 E. Shils, op. cit., p.11
16 Ibid.
17 *Aṅguttara-Nikāya* I, 10
18 E. Conze (trans.), *Buddhist Texts Through the Ages*, Bruno Cassirer, Oxford 1954, p.182
19 E. Shils, op. cit., p.11
20 S. Collins, *Selfless Persons*, Cambridge University Press, 1982, p.192
21 *Saṁyutta-Nikāya*, iii. 86
22 Bhikkhu Ñāṇamoli (trans.), *The Life of the Buddha*, Buddhist Publication Society, Kandy 1984, p.209
23 *Vinaya-Piṭaka* ii, 10
24 Raimondo Pannikar, *The Silence of God: The Answer of the Buddha*, Orbis, New York 1989, p.3
25 Sangharakshita, *The Ten Pillars of Buddhism*, Windhorse, third edition Glasgow 1989, pp.36–7
26 Dharmachari Tejananda, 'Faith, Devotion and Ritual', in *Puja and the Transformation of the Heart*, Windhorse, Glasgow 1987, p.20
27 Dharmachari Subhuti, *Buddhism For Today*, Windhorse, Glasgow 1988, p.60
28 In English alone. It has been translated into German, Swedish, Dutch, Finnish, Spanish, Hindi, Marathi, etc.
29 Sangharakshita (ed.) *The FWBO Puja Book: A Book of Buddhist Devotional Texts*, fifth edition, Windhorse, Glasgow 1990, p.8
30 Dharmachari Subhuti, op. cit., p.108
31 From my previously unpublished 'Letter to Dr Zaehner', printed as an appendix to this volume. *Vide supra* pp.181 *et seq.*
32 Ibid. p.184
33 *Brahmajāla-sutta, Dīgha-Nikāya* I
34 *The Vedanta Kesari*, Ramakrishna Mission, Madras 1948
35 Sangharakshita, *The Ten Pillars of Buddhism*, Windhorse, third edition Glasgow 1989, p.8
36 Sangharakshita, *Crossing the Stream*, Windhorse, Glasgow 1987, p.45

37 Ibid., pp.42–3
38 John Macquarrie, *Mary for all Christians*, Collins, London 1990, p.19
39 *Sigālovāda-sutta, Dīgha-Nikāya* XXXI
40 Stuart Miller, *Men and Friendship*, Gateway Books, London 1983, p.3
41 Ibid., p.4
42 Sangharakshita, *The Ten Pillars of Buddhism*, op. cit., p.72
43 Sangharakshita, *Vision and Transformation: An Introduction to the Buddha's Noble Eightfold Path*, Windhorse, Glasgow 1990, p.138
44 The Gospel According to St Mark, 3:21
45 Andy Gaus (trans.), *The Unvarnished Gospels*, Putney, Vermont 1988, p.76
46 See Sir Edwin Arnold's *The Light of Asia*, Book the Seventh, for a poetic version of this episode.
47 *Udāna* V.5
48 *Dhammapada* 348
49 Reported by Sanit Ekachai, 'Buddhism and Prostitution', *Bangkok Post*, 11 February 1991. Reprinted in *NIBWA Newsletter on International Buddhist Women's Activities* no.27 April–June 1991
50 Raymond Williams, *Culture and Society 1780–1950*, Penguin, 1979, p.17
51 Sangharakshita, *The History of My Going for Refuge*, Windhorse, Glasgow 1988, p.103 *et seq.*
52 Dharmachari Subhuti, op. cit., p.99
53 Malcolm Woodfield, op. cit. p.145
54 Ibid., p.183